Gainsborough's Blue Boy

The Return of a British Icon

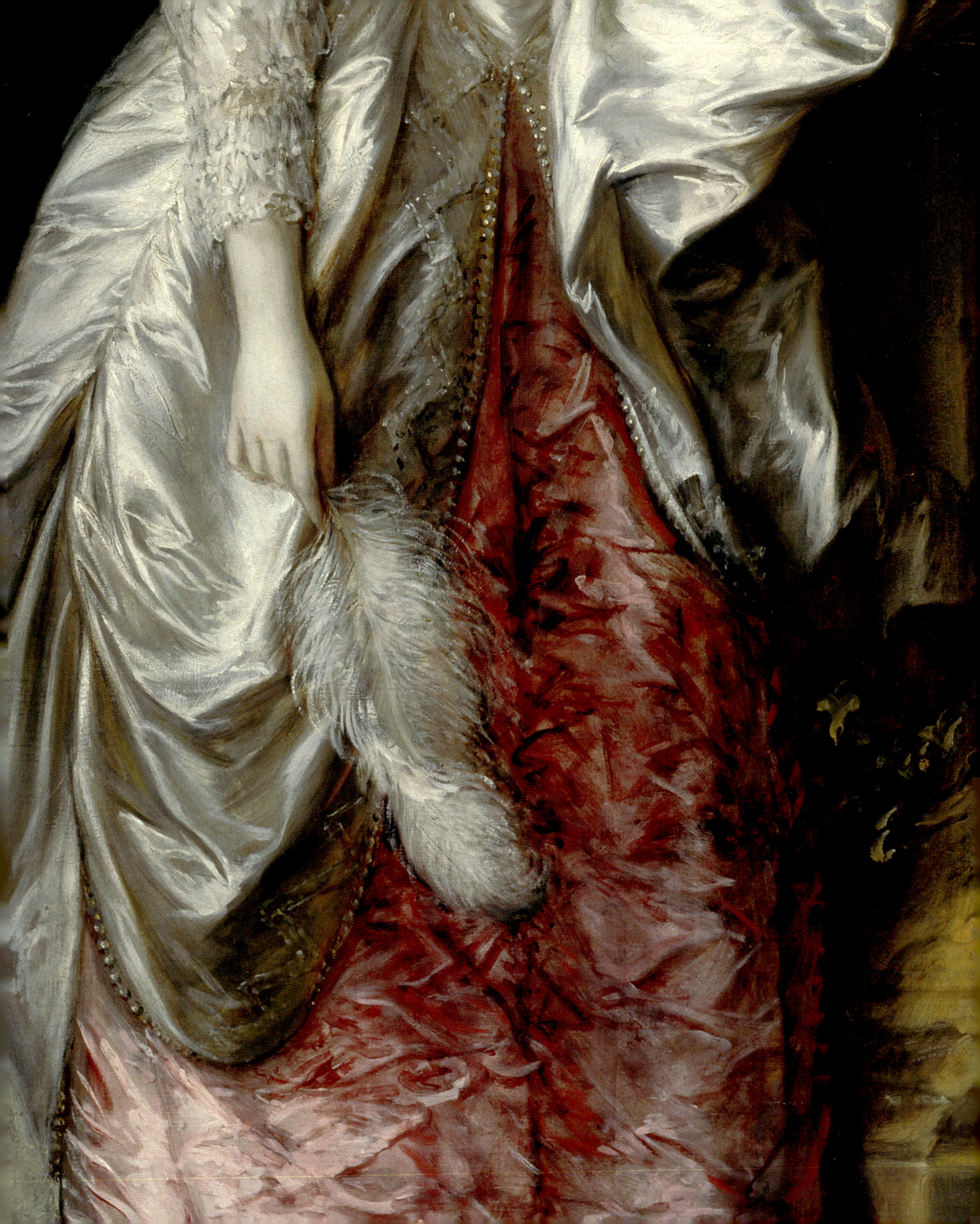

Gainsborough's Blue Boy

The Return of a British Icon

CHRISTINE RIDING

WITH CONTRIBUTIONS BY

SUSANNA AVERY-QUASH, MELINDA McCURDY, JACQUELINE RIDING AND IMOGEN TEDBURY

National Gallery Company, London
Distributed by Yale University Press

Published to accompany the exhibition

Gainsborough's Blue Boy

The National Gallery, London
25 January – 15 May 2022

Principal supporters

The H J Hyams Exhibition Programme
Supported by The Capricorn Foundation

The Sir John Ritblat Family Foundation

Funds for the conservation of Gainsborough's *The Blue Boy* were generously provided to The Huntington Library, Art Museum, and Botanical Gardens by the Bank of America Art Conservation Project

This exhibition has been made possible by the provision of insurance through the Government Indemnity Scheme. The National Gallery would like to thank HM Government for providing Government Indemnity and the Department for Digital, Culture, Media and Sport and Arts Council England for arranging the indemnity.

First published in 2022 by
National Gallery Company Limited
St Vincent House
30 Orange Street
London WC2H 7HH
www.nationalgallery.co.uk

ISBN 978 1 85709 680 4
1050981

British Library Cataloguing-in-Publication Data
A catalogue record is available from the British Library
Library of Congress Control Number 2021934159

All measurements give height before width

Publisher: Laura Lappin
Project Editor: Diana Adell
Editor: Rachel Giles
Designer: Joe Ewart
Picture Researchers: Suzanne Bosman and Rebecca Thornton
Production: Jane Hyne

Colour origination by DL
Printed in Belgium by Graphius

Front cover: Thomas Gainsborough, *The Blue Boy* (detail, cat. 1)
Back cover: Anthony van Dyck, *George Villiers, 2nd Duke of Buckingham (1628–1687) and Lord Francis Villiers (1629–1648)* (detail, cat. 5)
Page 2: Thomas Gainsborough, *The Hon. Mrs Graham* (detail, fig. 11)
Pages 50–1: Thomas Gainsborough, *The Painter's Daughters chasing a Butterfly* (detail, fig. 37)

On the occasion of this exhibition the following works were exhibited in Room 46 of the National Gallery, London: cats 1, 3, 4, 5 and 6.

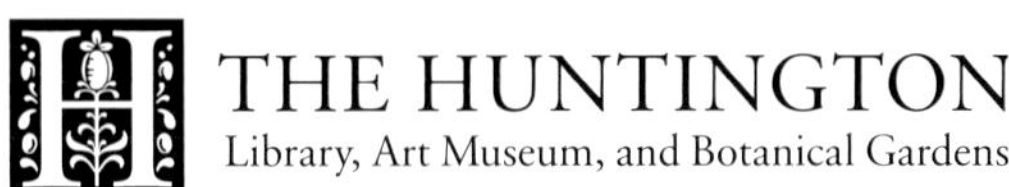

Contents

Forewords

For the last century The Huntington Library, Art Museum, and Botanical Gardens has been home to Thomas Gainsborough's *Blue Boy*, one of the most iconic old master paintings in the world. During this time, it has inspired the work of generations of artists; it has made cameos on television and in film; and it has been cherished by millions of museum visitors. As stewards of this extraordinary work, we recently completed a multi-year, public conservation project, the *Project Blue Boy*. Supported by generous funding from Bank of America, our Senior Paintings Conservator, Christina O'Connell, made invaluable discoveries that add to our knowledge of Gainsborough's revolutionary brushwork and his innovative experiments with a range of blue pigments that yielded astonishing effects.

Now, as we celebrate the 100th anniversary of *The Blue Boy*'s arrival in California, we are honoured to be partnering with the National Gallery on this once-in-a-lifetime opportunity to share the painting with appreciative audiences in the United Kingdom. In return, we will share with our own visitors the National Gallery's magisterial *Experiment on a Bird in the Airpump* (1768) by Joseph Wright 'of Derby' in an installation that also includes books and instruments from the Huntington Library's renowned History of Science collection.

We are grateful to National Gallery Director Gabriele Finaldi for his avid support in this endeavour and to National Gallery Curator Christine Riding for highlighting just what sets the *Blue Boy* painting apart, even within an august art-historical context. I would like to extend special thanks to the Huntington's Board of Trustees for their careful consideration and support of this project. I'm grateful to Art Museum Director Christina Nielsen, Sandra Brooke, Avery Director of the Library, who oversees the Huntington's conservation programme, and Rothenberg Vice-President Janet Albert, all of whom have helped to ensure the safe passage of this international treasure. Curator of British Art, Melinda McCurdy, and the entire Art Museum division have been diligent stewards of *The Blue Boy* while also emphasising its relevance to a wide range of audiences at home and abroad. Indeed, thanks go to generations of Huntington Trustees and staff who have cherished and protected *The Blue Boy* for 100 years.

Karen R. Lawrence, President
The Huntington Library, Art Museum,
and Botanical Gardens

In January 1922 Thomas Gainsborough's *Blue Boy* left Britain for the United States. One of the most celebrated pictures in the world and also, at that time, the most expensive, it was a trophy acquisition by the American railway magnate, Henry E. Huntington (1850–1927). But before it boarded an ocean liner for transportation to New York, *The Blue Boy* was exhibited at the National Gallery for three weeks where it was met with scenes bordering on hysteria. Some 90,000 people queued to see it and *The Times* reported that visitors were inclined to weep as they bade this beautiful boy farewell. The Director of the National Gallery at the time, Sir Charles Holmes, inscribed the words 'au revoir' on the reverse of the canvas – recent examination has confirmed that the inscription is still there – in the hope, perhaps, that the picture might be seen again in Britain.

One hundred years on, to the day, with a symmetry that befits the poise of the mysterious sitter, *The Blue Boy* is once again on display at the National Gallery, thanks to the extraordinary generosity of the Trustees of The Huntington Library, Art Museum, and Botanical Gardens, the institution established by Henry E. Huntington in San Marino, California. This time it is on show for 16 weeks.

Encapsulating to a unique degree the effortless aristocratic elegance of Van Dyck's 'grand manner' portraiture which Gainsborough so admired, *The Blue Boy* is also a piece of astounding bravura painting, a work of almost unbearable romantic nostalgia, an influential popular icon and much more besides, as the authors of this publication demonstrate in their essays. In California, it presides over a constellation of superb British paintings. At the National Gallery it takes its place among a distinguished succession of superb portraits by Holbein, Titian, Rembrandt, Velázquez, Van Dyck, Reynolds, Gainsborough himself and Thomas Lawrence, whose '*Red Boy*' was acquired for the nation just last year.

Initial discussions regarding the possible loan of *The Blue Boy* to London (it has never before been lent by the Huntington) were held in 2015 with Lord Rothschild and representatives of the Huntington, and we are delighted that the project has finally come to fruition. We have many people to thank for this special display at the National Gallery, beginning with our colleagues at the Huntington, especially Karen R. Lawrence, President of The Huntington Library, Art Museum, and Botanical Gardens; Christina Nielsen, Hannah and Russell Kully Director of the Art Museum; and in London, Christine Riding, the Jacob Rothschild Head of the Curatorial Department and Curator of British Paintings. We are grateful to the other lenders to the exhibition, Her Majesty the Queen and the Trustees of the Dulwich Picture Gallery. The exhibition is supported by The Capricorn Foundation, in memory of Mr H J Hyams, and we owe its trustees a continuing debt of gratitude. We are also most grateful to The Sir John Ritblat Family Foundation as a principal supporter of the exhibition.

Gabriele Finaldi, Director
The National Gallery, London

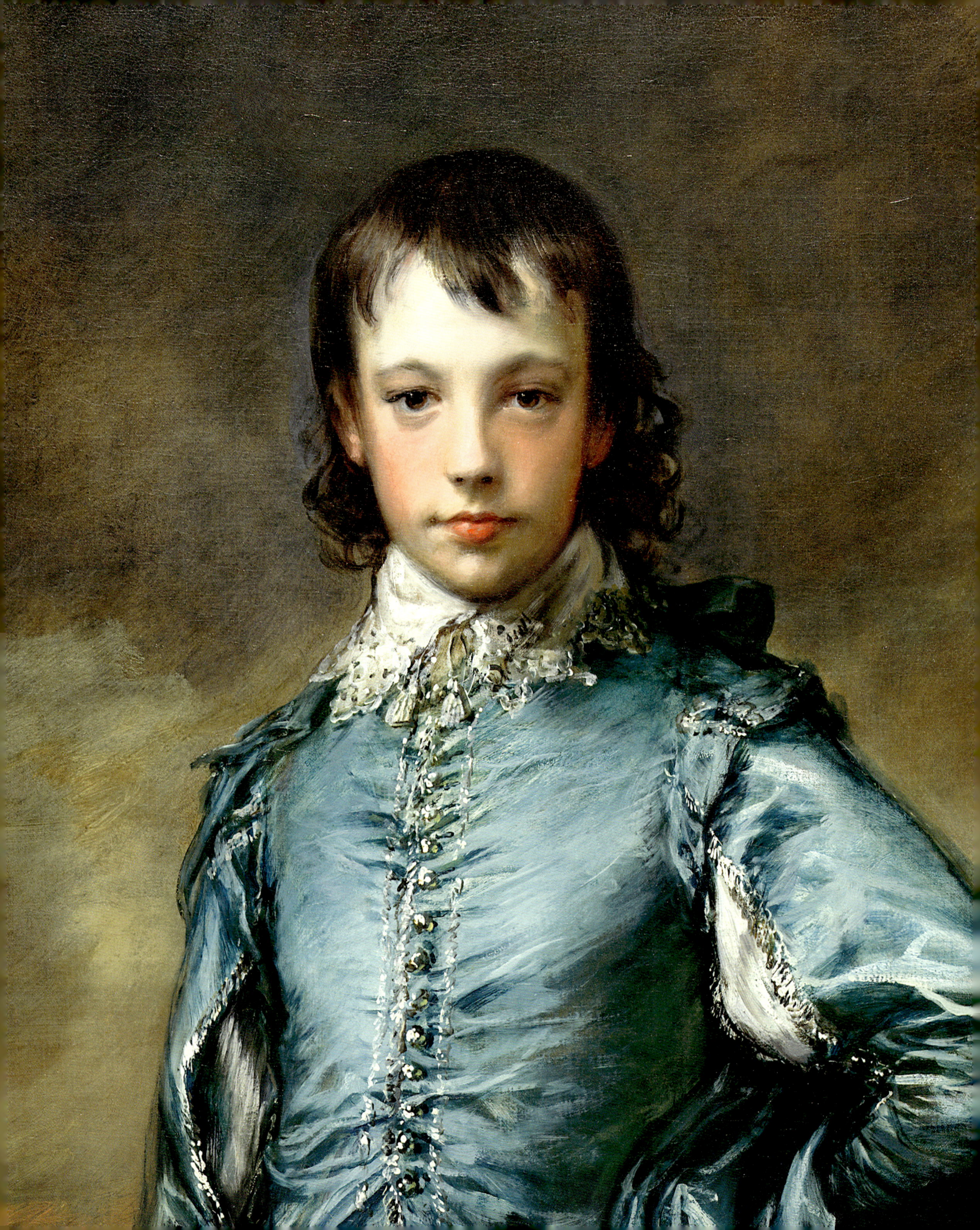

Van Dyck, Gainsborough and *The Blue Boy*

Christine Riding

One of the ironies of art history is that Thomas Gainsborough's *Blue Boy* (cat. 1) attracted little public attention (as far as contemporary sources relay) when it was first shown at the Royal Academy in 1770. Yet 150 years later, when it was sold to the American tycoon Henry E. Huntington, it was one of the most famous paintings in the world. This spectacular and enigmatic full-length portrait of a youth in Van Dyck dress was created during Gainsborough's time in Bath (1759–74), a period when the artist's style and practice changed dramatically in response to his patrons' tastes and expectations. Living there also gave him the opportunity to study the work of past masters. For a painter who did not travel abroad, such artistic encounters were crucial; in his case, Gainsborough benefited from studying and copying works in prestigious collections in Bath and nearby country houses – above all, those by the seventeenth-century Flemish artist Anthony van Dyck.

Gainsborough was keen at this time to establish himself within the contemporary British art world, to engage with the longer, broader tradition of European painting, and to explore a variety of artistic genres – portraiture, landscape and so-called 'fancy pictures' (scenes of everyday life with elements of imagination or storytelling). Additionally, he sought to develop his practice as a society portrait painter, taking fresh inspiration from Van Dyck, whose work was widely acknowledged as the epitome of that genre. When Van Dyck returned to London in 1632, his reputation was largely based on his religious subjects, most of which were in collections in Continental Europe. However, for British patrons, the artist and his studio created countless portraits which remained in private collections nationwide.[1] Van Dyck had consciously adapted his style of representation to suit the political and cultural agenda of his greatest patron, King Charles I, and his court: brushwork, pose, expression and colour arrangement were deftly combined to suggest attributes of power and control, but in a way that appeared innate and effortless to the individuals represented. It was precisely this alluring formula that Gainsborough made his own in *The Blue Boy*. Furthermore, Gainsborough and his contemporaries – keen to elevate the status of the artist in Britain – admired Van Dyck for what he represented in the round: as a painter, courtier, collector and connoisseur.[2]

That Gainsborough painted such an unadulterated homage to Van Dyck was thus entirely in keeping with contemporary taste and pervading attitudes to canonical old masters. But it was also remarkable, bearing in mind his practice and focus up to that point.

Detail of cat. 1

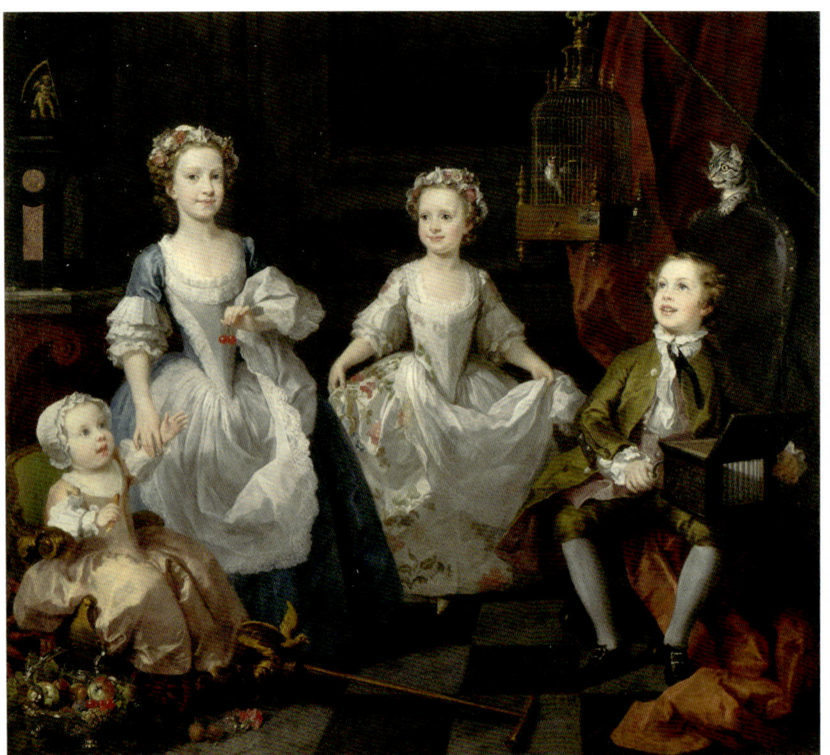

Fig. 1
William Hogarth (1697–1764)
The Graham Children, 1742
Oil on canvas, 160.5 × 181 cm
The National Gallery, London

Gainsborough had studied the old masters before moving to Bath. Indeed, while developing his first landscapes, he had looked to seventeenth-century Dutch painters, influences clearly reflected in his early masterpiece, *Cornard Wood, near Sudbury, Suffolk* (1748, National Gallery, London).[3] Yet his portraits and landscapes rarely quoted so overtly from European models, his primary focus being direct observation, with the objective (in the case of portraiture) of capturing a true and essential likeness. Even sitters in 'Van Dyck' costume – a vogue adopted as fancy dress for both popular entertainments and portraiture from the 1720s – had not been a priority for Gainsborough before 1770. In private correspondence of 1771, he even complained that classicising or masquerade costume would conceal, rather than reveal, the individual represented: 'Nothing can be more absurd than the foolish custom of Painters dressing people like scaramouches, and expecting the likeness to appear.'[4] So why did Gainsborough paint *The Blue Boy* in the way he did? And why did he submit the painting to public scrutiny at the newly instituted Royal Academy annual exhibition? Likely answers are complex, and, due to the paucity of extant contemporary evidence, speculative. Arguably, *The Blue Boy* encapsulates Gainsborough's artistic ethos, and reflects his promotion of an alternative Northern European lineage for British art to the Classical, Italian tradition hitherto championed so widely, above all by Sir Joshua Reynolds in his influential role as the first President of Britain's Royal Academy.

Gainsborough relocated to the cosmopolitan spa town of Bath in 1759, primarily to cement his reputation as a leading portraitist. To match this ambition and to tempt a discerning urban clientele, he leased a series of well-appointed properties, which served simultaneously, according to the eighteenth-century convention, as a gentleman's home, a commodious studio for sitters, and a showroom in which visitors could admire his latest works.[5] Such an attention-grabbing image as *The Blue Boy* was probably painted for display in Gainsborough's second premises in the recently completed Circus, designed by the leading English architect John Wood.[6] Originally called 'King's Circus', this new address was a fitting setting for such a Van Dyckian picture because it formed part of Wood's vision for a cityscape based on the Palladian style, itself associated with the early Stuart period in England and the work of royal architect and designer Inigo Jones.[7]

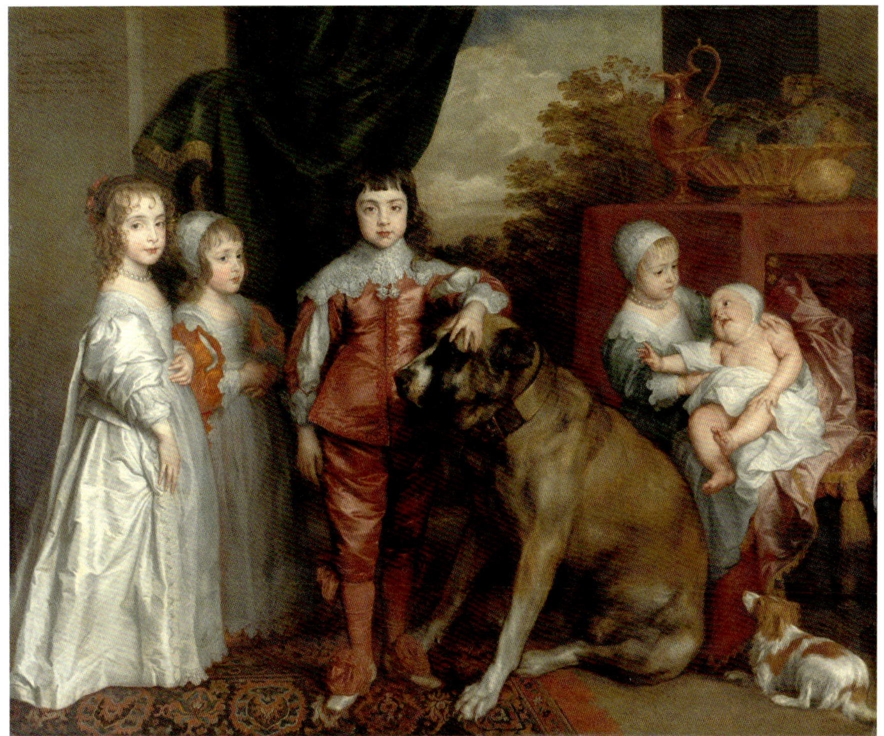

Fig. 2
Anthony van Dyck (1599–1641)
The Five Eldest Children of Charles I, 1637
Oil on canvas, 163.2 × 198.8 cm
The Royal Collection / HM Queen Elizabeth II

Gainsborough had started painting full-length portraits in the mid-1750s.[8] Earlier, during his time in London and Sudbury in the 1740s, his portrait style reflected the work of his contemporaries Francis Hayman, Hubert Gravelot and William Hogarth, who had been influenced by French painters including Jean-Antoine Watteau, Philippe Mercier and Jean-Baptiste-Siméon Chardin, who, in turn, had adapted seventeenth-century Dutch and Flemish traditions.[9] Many of Gainsborough's portraits during this period followed the then fashionable 'conversation pieces' (small-scale group portraits with full-length figures) that evolved from French *fêtes galantes* (an outdoor entertainment or rural festival), which suited Gainsborough's well-documented enthusiasm for landscape painting. While his painting of himself and his wife, Margaret (1746, Musée du Louvre, Paris) embraces Watteau and the French 'Rococo' style, his now celebrated portrait of local Essex gentry *Mr and Mrs Andrews* (fig. 34) represents a distillation of wider influences. Combining French and Dutch modes alongside the topographical tradition that celebrated land and estate ownership, Gainsborough was able to create an image that has since been described as quintessentially English.[10]

From the late 1740s, Gainsborough utilised his family and acquaintances as sitters and subjects to experiment with larger formats, looser brushwork and different genres.[11] The most innovative example shows his daughters, Margaret and Mary, outdoors chasing a butterfly (fig. 37). In contrast with his more decorous earlier group portrait, *The Artist with his Wife and Daughter* (about 1748, National Gallery, London), the handling of paint is much freer, mirroring the sense of spontaneity in the figures. The major transition to large-scale portraiture that was so vital for his career, both in terms of attracting the most affluent patrons and gaining him privileged access to their art collections, once more spoke of his indebtedness to those artists in Hogarth's circle. The paintings created for the Foundling Hospital in the 1740s and 1750s, for example, included not only Gainsborough's highly original view painting *The Charterhouse* (1748), but also two grand, and for the history of British art, signature portraits, *Captain Thomas Coram* (1740) by Hogarth and *Dr Richard Mead* (1747) by Allan Ramsay. Admittedly, Ramsay's imposing and authoritative representation of Mead, royal physician and renowned art collector,

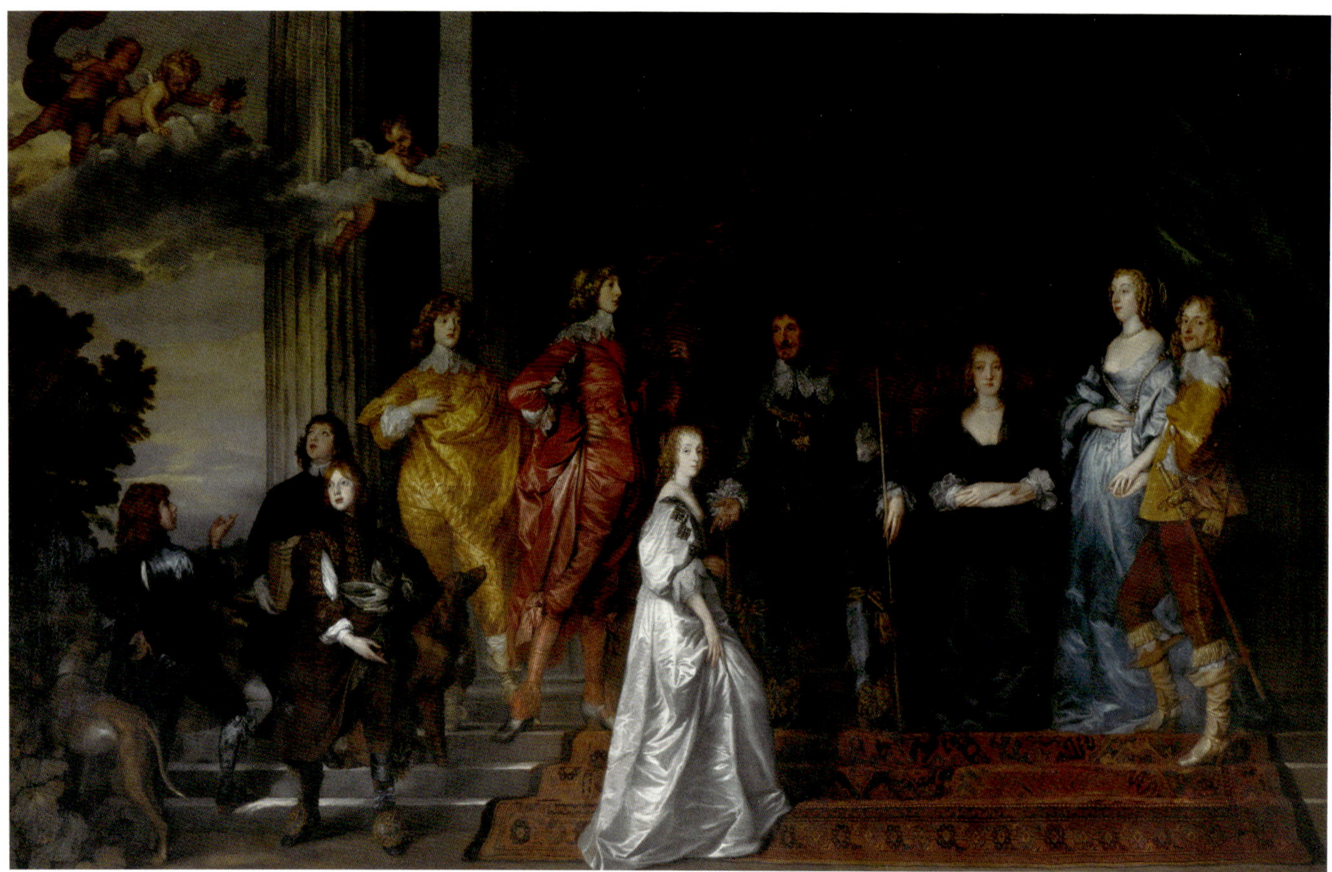

Fig. 3
Anthony van Dyck (1599–1641)
Philip Herbert, 4th Earl of Pembroke, with his Family, about 1635
Oil on canvas, 330 × 510 cm
Earl of Pembroke and Trustees of Wilton House

was more in tune with contemporary expectations. By contrast, Hogarth's likeness portrayed a charitable elderly shipwright, dressed informally. According to Hogarth, his portrait of Coram resulted from a challenge to fellow artists to join him in his emulation of Van Dyck,[12] while proving how the conventions of courtly portraiture could imbue even the most unlikely sitter with individuality and dignity.[13]

Hogarth had, tellingly, been trading under the 'Sign of the Golden Head' (a bust of none other than Van Dyck) at his Leicester Fields house since 1733, and his assimilation of European traditions within his portraiture of the 1740s and 1750s was evident especially in his life-size portraits of *The Graham Children* (fig. 1) and *The Mackinnon Children* (1742–3, National Gallery of Ireland, Dublin).[14] The former is of particular interest here, as it has been suggested that Hogarth's model may have been Van Dyck's *Five Eldest Children of Charles I* (fig. 2).[15] Both images show the different stages of childhood, the eldest child directly engaging with the viewer, while the attention of their younger siblings is distracted. Given the Graham family's long-standing connection to the British monarchy, as royal apothecaries, the resonance of Hogarth's portrait and its old master borrowings were not simply related to artistic concerns but were fitting and appreciated by the client.

Clearly Gainsborough was exposed to Van Dyck's influence before moving to Bath. However, commentators have long associated a major shift in his style with the opportunities offered in the West

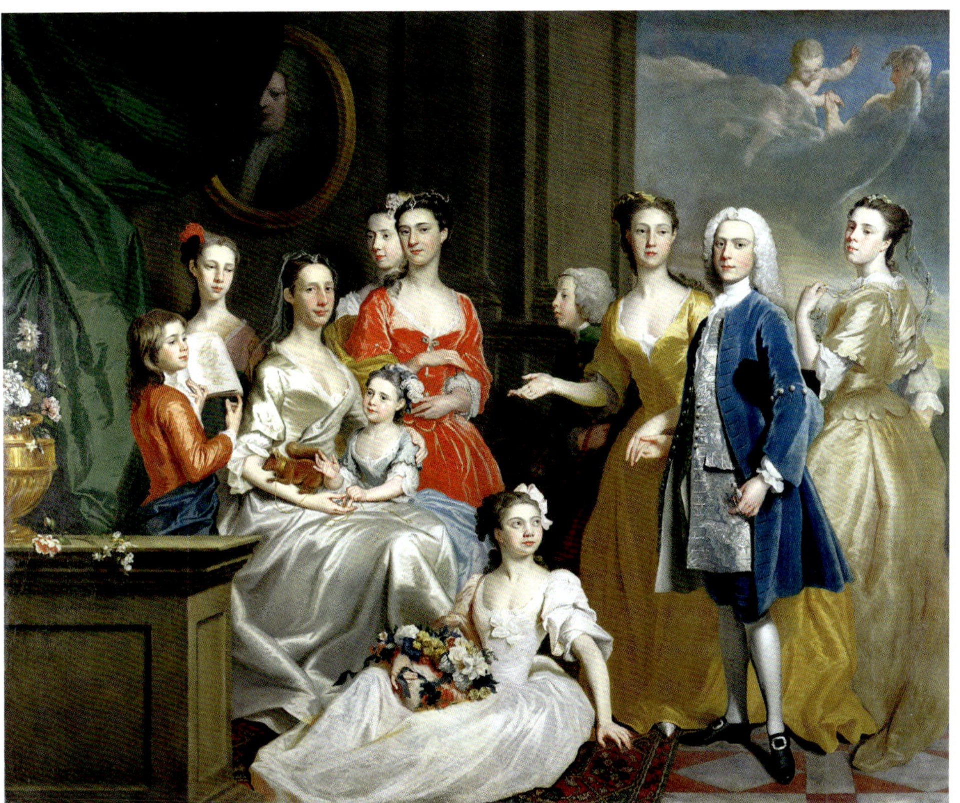

Fig. 4
Joseph Highmore (1692–1780)
The Family of Sir Eldred Lancelot Lee, 1736
Oil on canvas, 232 × 287 cm
Wolverhampton Art Gallery. Purchased with assistance of the Victoria and Albert Museum Purchase Grant Fund and the National Art Collections Fund, 1984

Country for studying notable art collections and the work of Van Dyck in particular.[16] Gainsborough visited Wilton House, for instance, in 1764, and there encountered Van Dyck's vast and celebrated portrait of Philip Herbert, 4th Earl of Pembroke with his family (fig. 3). To add to the spectacle, the 'Great Room', where this painting hung, was embellished with other portraits, including of Charles I and his wife, Henrietta Maria, all by Van Dyck – a demonstration of virtuosity that would have impressed any aspiring portraitist keen to emulate the Flemish master's artistic and social success.[17] The influence of the Pembroke family portrait on British art was widespread and lasting. As examples, both the vibrant and contrasting colours and the variety of poses and gestures in Joseph Highmore's *The Family of Sir Eldred Lancelot Lee* of 1736 (fig. 4) and Reynolds's *The Family of the Duke of Marlborough* of 1778 (Blenheim Palace) are indebted to Van Dyck's masterpiece.[18]

Van Dyck's artistic reputation across Europe was consolidated through the circulation of printed reproductions from the seventeenth century. An important initiative was the series of prints after his portraits, known as the *Iconographie*, which comprised likenesses of many famous crowned heads, military figures, scholars and artists of the time. That Van Dyck – who was knighted by Charles I and the first artist to be appointed 'Principal Painter in Ordinary to their Majesties' – included himself in the series was bold proof that artists too might achieve social equality with the foremost nobility. Unsurprisingly, the volume became an invaluable resource for painters for over two hundred years, in terms of aspirations concerning their standing as much as ideas for their art.[19]

While Gainsborough made copies after Peter Paul Rubens, David Teniers the Younger and Rembrandt, Van Dyck absorbed most of his interest from the 1760s.[20] In addition to making sketches and copies of *The Pembroke Family*, Gainsborough produced a highly finished version at scale (fig. 5) of *Lord John Stuart and his Brother, Lord Bernard Stuart* (cat. 4).[21] These copies functioned as studies in technique, composition and subject matter, as well as declarations to current and future patrons of the artist's skill, knowledge and taste. As such, they formed

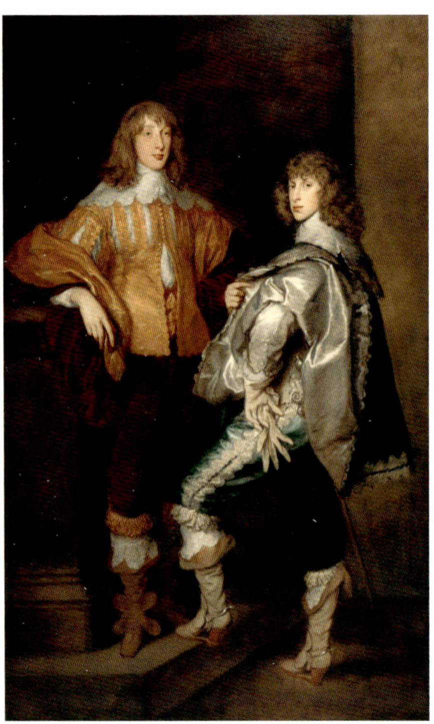

an integral part of the semi-public displays in the artist's studio-cum-showroom, alongside paintings of Gainsborough's own devising. Given that many of these copies remained with Gainsborough until his death, we can imagine *The Blue Boy* displayed first in fashionable Palladian-style premises in Bath, and then, after his move to London in 1774, at Schomberg House, an elegant seventeenth-century building on Pall Mall, amidst his own copies of Van Dyck's portraits of the Stuart brothers (fig. 5), Inigo Jones, and possibly a (now lost) version of Charles I's children.[22]

While building his practice and reputation in Bath, Gainsborough actively sought to make himself visible in London, pitting his work against his contemporaries through the novel forum, for British artists at least, of contemporary art exhibitions. From 1761 to 1768, he sent 16 portraits (and three landscapes) to the Society of Artists, most of which were full-lengths, each underscoring his growing confidence in assimilating artistic conventions, past and present, in a thoroughly contemporary manner.[23] The portrait of the actor James Quin (1763, National Gallery of Ireland, Dublin) reveals Gainsborough's canny exploitation of celebrities as a means of drawing attention to his work in crowded exhibition venues while eschewing the practice of painters such as Johan Zoffany, Reynolds and occasionally Hogarth, who depicted actors in role or allegorical guise. Quin is shown as a gentleman in contemporary dress, holding a book of plays, with a bust of Shakespeare, to indicate his former profession and intellectual standing.[24] Only the year before, Reynolds had shown his *David Garrick between the Muses of Tragedy and Comedy* (1760–1, Waddesdon Manor, Buckinghamshire) at the Society of Artists, which made overt reference to seventeenth-century works such as *Drunken Silenus Supported by Satyrs* (about 1620, National Gallery, London), a painting then thought to be by Rubens although now associated with his most gifted pupil, Van Dyck.[25] The relative stance of both artists in relation to portraiture was only reinforced by Gainsborough exhibiting his very different portrait of Garrick in 1766. As with Quin, Gainsborough depicted him in contemporary dress with a bust of Shakespeare, at ease in a landscape setting. This stark contrast in artistic approach, played out in the public sphere, can once more be seen in Gainsborough's glamorous portrait of the actress Sarah Siddons (cat. 6), which melds contemporary modishness with Van Dyckian overtones. This was painted the year after Reynolds exhibited to great acclaim his own *Sarah Siddons as the Tragic Muse* at the Royal Academy (fig. 38), which weaves in a gamut of old master and literary allusions, not least a reference to Michelangelo's enthroned figures from the Sistine Chapel ceiling.[26]

At the same time as these portraits of public figures, Gainsborough continued to use family members as models to refresh and extend his output. These included the more formal portrait of his daughters as art students, a painting that signals his ongoing engagement with Van Dyck (fig. 36; cat. 4). A different tone is struck by *Margaret Gainsborough Gleaning* (about 1760–1, Ashmolean Museum, Oxford), a 'fancy painting' featuring Gainsborough's daughter as a rural worker, and the so-called *Pitminster Boy* of the late 1760s (private collection),

Fig. 5
Thomas Gainsborough (1727–1788)
after Anthony van Dyck (1599–1641)
Lords John and Bernard Stuart,
about 1760–70
Oil on canvas, 235 × 146.1 cm
Saint Louis Art Museum. Gift of Mrs. Jackson Johnson in memory of Mr. Jackson Johnson

Fig. 6
Thomas Gainsborough (1727–1788)
Isabella, Viscountess Molyneux, later Countess of Sefton, 1769
Oil on canvas, 236 × 155 cm
Walker Art Gallery, Liverpool. Presented to the Walker Art Gallery by HM Government in 1975

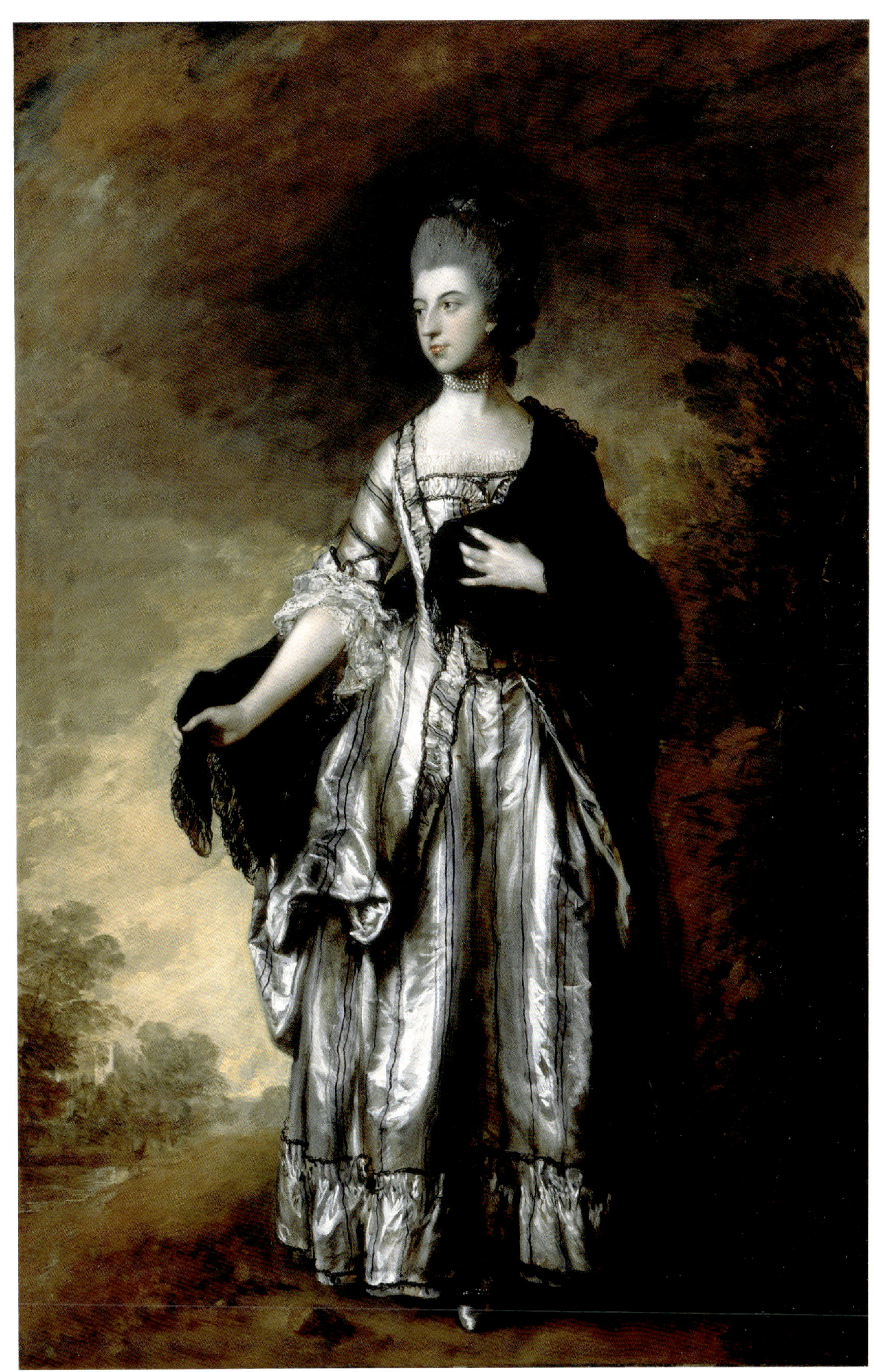

which represents one of his studio assistants, waiting to hand him a brush. Rather than a straightforward portrait sketch, the latter has been described as a 'study of expression', in the manner of seventeenth-century Dutch *tronies* (heads).[27] Gainsborough clearly rated it, as it appears to be his submission, described as 'A boy's head', to the inaugural exhibition of the Royal Academy in 1769. If this is so, it accompanied his full-length portrait of Isabella, Viscountess Molyneux (fig. 6), whose dominant figure, low horizon and idealised landscape setting foreshadows *The Blue Boy*, as does the contrast between the warm natural tones of the background and the cool colours of her contemporary dress.[28] Importantly, too, it is closer to seventeenth-century prototypes, by Van Dyck and Rubens specifically, than any portrait Gainsborough had hitherto created. The erect nobility of the pose and remote, inscrutable expression are in direct contrast to the ease and sense of individuality of his earlier full-length female portraits, starting with that of the professional musician Ann Ford of 1760 (Cincinnati Art Museum).[29] Looking at Gainsborough's four submissions to the Royal Academy in 1769 – two single full-length portraits, a large landscape and a fancy picture – we can surmise that his strategy was to demonstrate his versatility across genres and ability to assimilate a range of old master traditions to elevate his art without, however, resorting to the 'timeless' costume and accoutrements of classical tradition, deployed by such rivals as Reynolds and George Romney.[30]

The following year, Gainsborough exhibited *The Blue Boy*, which pushed these experiments yet further. It was described in the catalogue (according to the convention of the time, which favoured anonymity) as 'Portrait of a young gentleman'. Unlike his other portraits, where the sitters' identities have been established, that of *The Blue Boy* remains speculative. It was long held to be Jonathan Buttall, a former owner of the painting, and son of a London ironmonger. Recently, however, it has been suggested that the sitter was Gainsborough's nephew and only student, Gainsborough Dupont, who may have sat for *The Pitminster Boy* and who like his younger cousin, Edward Richard Gardner, certainly posed in the same blue Van Dyck dress for other paintings by Gainsborough before and after 1770 (fig. 7). With the sitter cast as a Stuart nobleman, *The Blue Boy* is a masterclass in pictorial social mobility, which surely helps to explain its enduring appeal, not least to viewers whose own social status was unconventional or unestablished. Taking this idea further, the fact that Gainsborough reused a canvas (proving that *The Blue Boy* was not a commissioned work) more than hints that the identity of the sitter was comparatively unimportant, and that rather he was interested in creating a new kind of masterpiece, a Van Dyck painting for the modern age, at once incorporating elements of portrait, landscape and fancy picture.

The Blue Boy speaks particularly to Van Dyck's portraits of youths, *George Villiers, 2nd Duke of Buckingham and Lord Francis Villiers* (cat. 5) and *The Five Eldest Children of Charles I* (fig. 2). The latter, a less often remarked-on comparison, has arguably stronger resonances, not least the arresting frontal pose and expression of the future Charles II, at

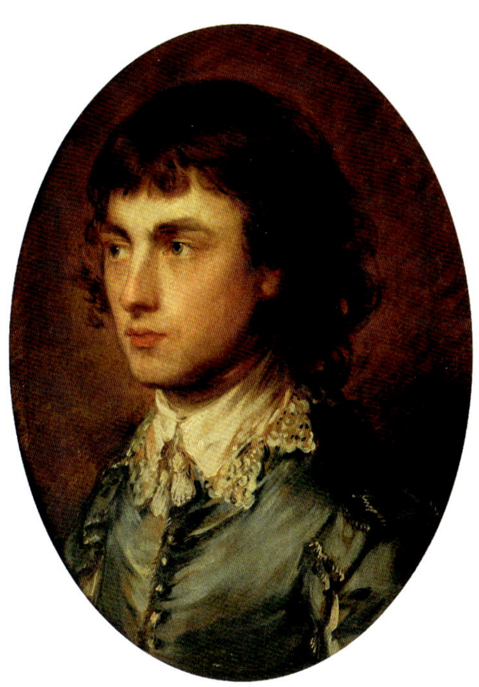

Fig. 7
Thomas Gainsborough (1727–1788)
Gainsborough Dupont, 1773
Oil on canvas, 51.6 × 38.8 cm
Waddesdon (Rothschild Family)

the centre of the composition. There is also much in the painterly process and technique which unites both paintings with *The Blue Boy*. During his so-called 'English period' when Van Dyck painted the royal children, his brushwork became less visible, facial expressions simpler and clearer, the costumes dominated by one or two striking and contrasting colours. This greater paring down to essentials allows the eye to fix on Van Dyck's painterly interpretation of luxurious materials, just as the viewer does when confronting Gainsborough's *Blue Boy*.[31] With Van Dyck's work in mind, was Gainsborough seeking to create a generalised vision of 'youth', whose beauty and poise, complementing the virtuosic technique and bold composition, evoked and invoked his greatest artistic mentor, Van Dyck?

That suggestion provokes another question: how does *The Blue Boy* sit with other eighteenth-century portraits in Van Dyck dress? Most commentators link this distinct theme in British portraiture to the vogue for masquerade dress, particularly costume associated with the court of Charles I.[32] In fact, there are other reasons for the adoption of such dress, which relate to the Flemish painter's multi-faceted legacy. The Van Dyck dress used in Reynolds's portrait of David Garrick (1768, Royal Collection), in the role of Kitely from Ben Jonson's *Every Man in his Humour* (1598), is as anachronistic as that deployed in Peter Scheemakers's influential Shakespeare monument, installed in Westminster Abbey's 'Poet's Corner' in 1741. The appropriation of Van Dyck dress in British literary and theatrical life only underscores the symbiotic relationship between the theatre and art worlds, in terms of profile and self-promotion, and that both forms of artistic expression were performances. Paintings were routinely described as such at the time, not simply because they utilised poses, props and costumes, but the very 'act' of painting itself.[33] The masquerade, with its focus on disguise and role play, is integral to this theme, a theatrical innovation linked to the wealth and politics of the early Stuart period in England. Here it is pertinent to recall that a novelty in British art attributed to Van Dyck is the use of idealised 'Arcadian' landscapes, which originated in part in the scenery designed by Inigo Jones and others for court masques.[34] Such traditions find echoes in Gainsborough's approach to *The Blue Boy*, which is nothing if not a self-conscious 'performance' of style, pose and setting.

Van Dyck was also a distinguished collector and connoisseur. Among the prestigious Italian pictures that he brought to London were Titian's *Vendramin Family* (about 1540–5, National Gallery, London) and *Perseus and Andromeda* (1554–6, The Wallace Collection, London). Van Dyck admired Titian more than any other artist, a passion he shared with Charles I, who, in turn, regarded Van Dyck as the living embodiment of the Renaissance artist.[35] Moreover, the Stuart king's reputation as the most discerning art collector ever to occupy a British throne was largely based on his enthusiasm for classical sculpture and medals, Italian Renaissance art, and his patronage of Rubens, Van Dyck, Bernini and other eminent European artists: in short, the very foundations of the cultural phenomenon known as the Grand Tour that took the sons of the aristocracy and gentry on extended tours of

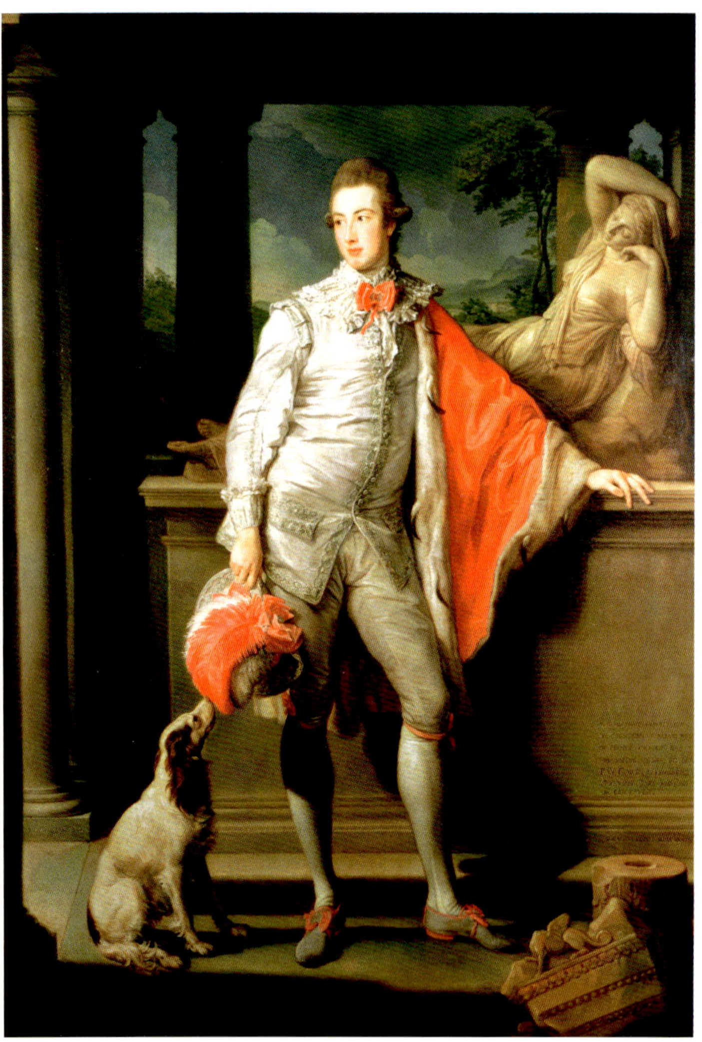

Fig. 8
Pompeo Batoni (1708–1787)
Thomas William Coke, later 1st Earl of Leicester of the Second Creation, 1773–4
Oil on canvas, 245.8 × 170.3 cm
The Earl of Leicester and the Trustees of the Holkham Estate

Europe, above all Italy.[36] Hence the adoption of Van Dyck dress in eighteenth-century Grand Tour portraiture, a preeminent example of which is *Thomas William Coke* by Pompeo Batoni of 1773–4 (fig. 8). This is not merely fanciful but calculated to draw on the cultural authority of Charles I and Van Dyck. Reynolds, who promoted the idea of Continental travel as vital to artistic development and had conducted his own Grand Tour in the 1750s, was painted by Angelica Kauffman in 1767 (Saltram House, Devon) as a cultured and intellectual man in Van Dyck dress.[37] He sits leaning on a table, piled with treatises, periodicals and an engraving of an antique sculpture, alongside a bust of Michelangelo, an artist whom Reynolds revered.

In comparison, *The Blue Boy* seems almost liberated from such loaded trappings, thus representing a kind of declaration of independence. Gainsborough never travelled abroad or gained a reputation as a collector, just as he eschewed the company of Royal Academicians or Reynolds's literary associates.[38] But he affirmed his gentility in other ways, not least in relation to his wife's family: Margaret was the illegitimate only daughter of Henry, 3rd Duke of Beaufort, from whom she received an annuity. Furthermore, Gainsborough was a gifted musician and moved in elite musical circles, as witnessed by his striking portraits of leading composers and performers including his *Elizabeth and Mary Linley* (cat. 3).[39] Such a lifestyle allowed him to present himself as a man of culture, as demonstrated by his sensitive interpretation of Van Dyck in *The Blue Boy*.

With the start of a new reign in 1760, the relationship between Van Dyck and the Stuart monarchy offered another model for British artists. Numerous painters enjoyed the patronage of George III and Queen Charlotte, particularly Ramsay, Zoffany, Benjamin West and eventually Gainsborough himself, and the portraits commissioned by the royal couple during the 1760s include some with a distinct Van Dyck/Stuart focus, such as Zoffany's *George III, Queen Charlotte and their Six Eldest Children* (fig. 9) and *George, Prince of Wales, and Frederick, later Duke of York, at Buckingham House* of 1765 (Royal Collection). The latter shows the two boys in a room displayed with Van Dyck's portrait of the Villiers brothers (cat. 5) and *The Three Eldest Children of Charles I* (1635–6, Royal Collection). In the same year, George III acquired Van Dyck's *Five Eldest Children of Charles I* (fig. 2), an indication of the Hanoverian dynasty's admiration for and sense of kinship with the early Stuarts and the aesthetic of the Caroline court. With its direct relationship to the Van Dycks mentioned here, *The Blue Boy* would have

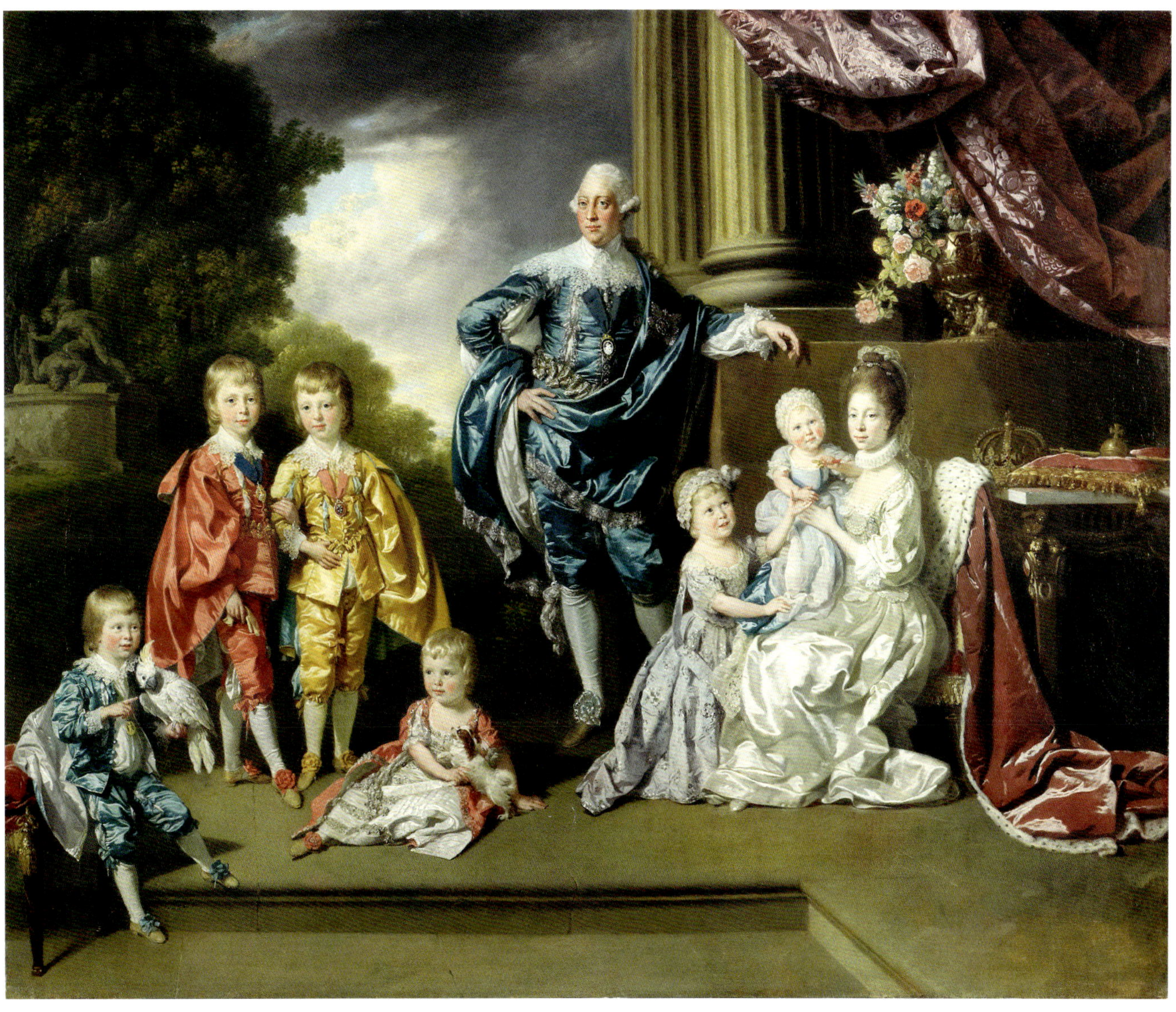

Fig. 9
Johan Joseph Zoffany (1733–1810)
George III, Queen Charlotte and their Six Eldest Children, 1770
Oil on canvas, 104.9 × 127.4 cm
The Royal Collection / HM Queen Elizabeth II

been an eloquent advertisement for Gainsborough in his pursuit of royal favour, especially given that Zoffany's portrait of the royal family in Van Dyck dress was also at the 1770 Royal Academy exhibition.[40]

Interestingly, it has been recently argued that Van Dyck dress was linked to Jacobitism and the enduring loyalty to the senior and Catholic branch of the Stuart dynasty which promoted Prince Charles Edward Stuart as the legitimate heir to the British throne, and that such sentiments existed among Gainsborough's clientele in Bath and beyond (see pp. 34–5).[41] This idea only adds to the potential subversiveness of *The Blue Boy*, painted 14 years or so after the Jacobite Rebellion of 1745–6, arguably the greatest domestic threat to the Hanoverian dynasty.[42] Yet George III's interest in Van Dyck's imagery was also a means of visually underscoring his direct descent from James I and Charles I. Furthermore, since Van Dyck painted the royal family as an interconnected group, with the children newly

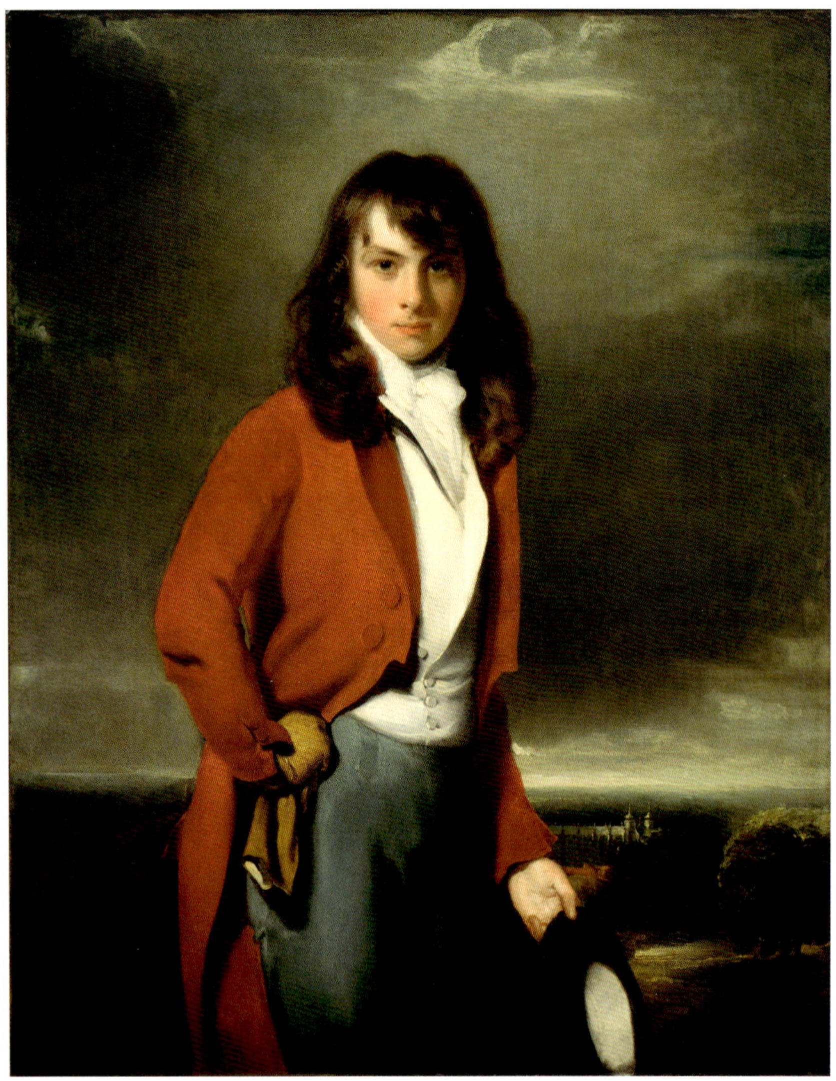

Fig. 10
Thomas Lawrence (1769–1830)
Portrait of Arthur Atherley as an Etonian, 1791–2
Oil on canvas, 125.7 × 100.3 cm
Los Angeles County Museum of Art. Gift of Hearst Magazines

represented as noble, cherished and childlike, George III and Queen Charlotte may have wished to demonstrate their own espousal of values associated with Charles and Henrietta Maria as dutiful, loving parents, as well as imply dynastic unity, continuity and permanence.[43]

Unlike Reynolds, Gainsborough did not achieve a formal position at court, but he was the preferred painter to the royal family in the 1780s. His full-length portrait of Queen Charlotte (Royal Collection) was exhibited at the Royal Academy in 1781, and the following year he was represented by a series of 15 head-and-shoulder portraits of the royal family (1782, Royal Collection), the last year he participated at the annual exhibition. His *Three Eldest Princesses* (relating to Van Dyck's admired portrait, mentioned above) was displayed at Gainsborough's London home, Schomberg House, between 1784 and 1786.[44] In turn, Gainsborough's vivacious and graceful likenesses were exemplars to the next generation of painters. A prime example of artistic emulation is Thomas Lawrence's portrait of Queen Charlotte (1789, National Gallery, London), painted the year after Gainsborough's death and exhibited at the Royal Academy in 1790, alongside another virtuosic portrait equally indebted to him, *Elizabeth Farren, Later Countess of Derby* (1790, Metropolitan Museum of Art). Lawrence's striking portrait of the twenty-year-old Arthur Atherley (fig. 10), exhibited the year of Reynolds's death in 1792, equally affirms the young artist as the heir to both him and Gainsborough, and by extension Van Dyck and other old masters.[45]

While the sitter's identity has preoccupied commentators, a persistent myth linked to *The Blue Boy* is that it was painted as a rebuff to Reynolds, thereby potentially acting as a kind of lightning rod for areas of disagreement and divergence between artists from the early days of the Royal Academy onwards. The specific circumstance was first recorded in 1820 by John Young, the cataloguer of the Duke of Westminster collection, who assumed that *The Blue Boy* was 'painted in consequence of a dispute between Gainsborough, Sir Joshua Reynolds, and several other artists. The former having asserted that he [Gainsborough] thought the predominant colour in the Picture ought to be blue.'[46] What is interesting in this quotation is that the 'dispute' involved 'several other artists' too, thus suggesting a wider debate, rather than just a personal rivalry.[47]

As the legend goes, Reynolds had set out the opposite position to Gainsborough in his *Eighth Discourse* (1778), in a section devoted to the discussion of 'the means of producing that great effect which we observe in the works of the Venetian painters'.[48] He argues that 'the masses of light in a picture [should] be always of a warm mellow colour, yellow, red, or a yellowish-white; and that the blue, the grey, or the green colours be kept almost entirely out of these masses, and be used only to support and set off these warm colours; and for this purpose, a small proportion of cold colours will be sufficient.'[49] Reversing this principle 'to make a picture splendid and harmonious' would, according to Reynolds, be beyond the skill of even Rubens or Titian. However, the painting Reynolds specifically refers to as demonstrating his point is Titian's *Bacchus and Ariadne* (1520–3, National Gallery, London), a painting 'celebrated' for its 'harmony of colouring'. Here, the Venetian painter's superior colour management, Reynolds opines, when contrasted with that of Van Dyck and the Flemish school, results in the latter seeming 'cold and grey.'[50]

As has often been stated, Gainsborough's *Blue Boy* was exhibited some years before Reynolds's remarks to the Academy, although this specific issue on colour might have been circulating beforehand.[51] Indeed, the earliest observations about *The Blue Boy* were from professional painters, starting with an unidentified British draughtsman, who made a detailed drawing of the painting (1770, Victoria and Albert Museum), and a founding member of the Royal Academy, Mary Moser, who wrote to the Swiss artist Henry Fuseli in July 1770 that 'Gainsborough was beyond himself in the portrait of a gentleman in a Van Dyke [sic] habit'. Published later were the remarks of Francis Hayman, who died in 1776, but who evidently saw the painting, stating, 'What an extraordinary picture Gainsborough had painted of the *Blue Boy*; it is as fine as Vandyke [sic].'[52]

In his *Seventh Discourse* (1776), Reynolds praised the virtue of adopting classical dress for its simplicity and timelessness, but condemned Van Dyck dress and other 'whimsical capricious forms': 'We all very well remember,' he mused, 'how common it was a few years ago for portraits to be drawn in this fantastic dress; and this custom is not entirely laid aside.' As a result, he concluded, 'very ordinary pictures acquired something of the air and affect of the works of Vandyck, and appeared therefore at first sight to be better pictures than they really were'.[53] Reynolds had himself painted sitters, including youths, in Van Dyck dress and would continue to do so (see cat. 1). Clearly he made a distinction between theory and practice, here speaking as president and polemicist of the Academy, privileging the classical as intellectually 'high-minded'. Given Reynolds's well-known stance, aligning the British School with the training, attitudes and hierarchy of artistic genres of Continental Europe, the 'stay at-home' Gainsborough made quite a statement submitting *The Blue Boy* at the second-ever Royal Academy exhibition. And he was happy to make

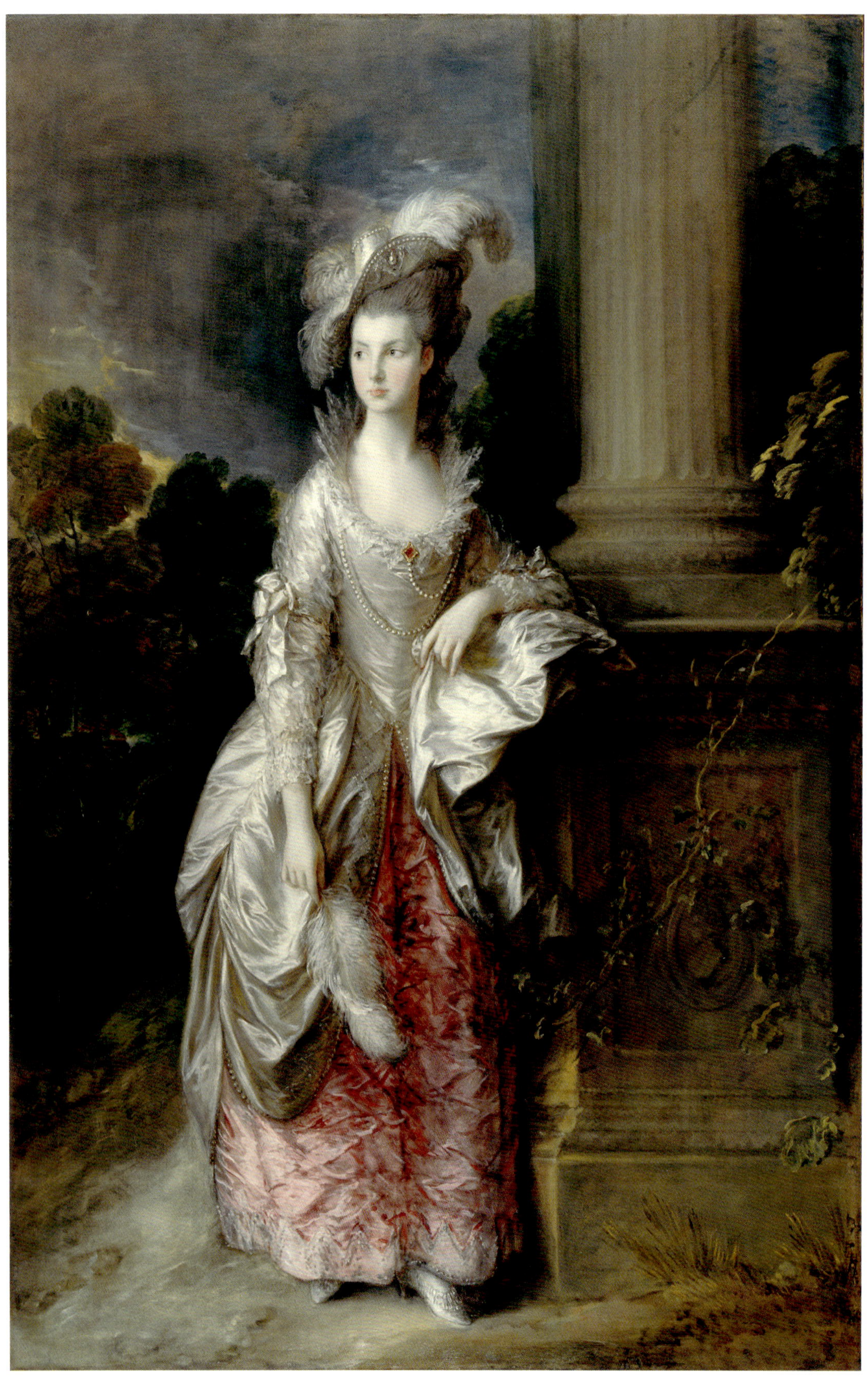

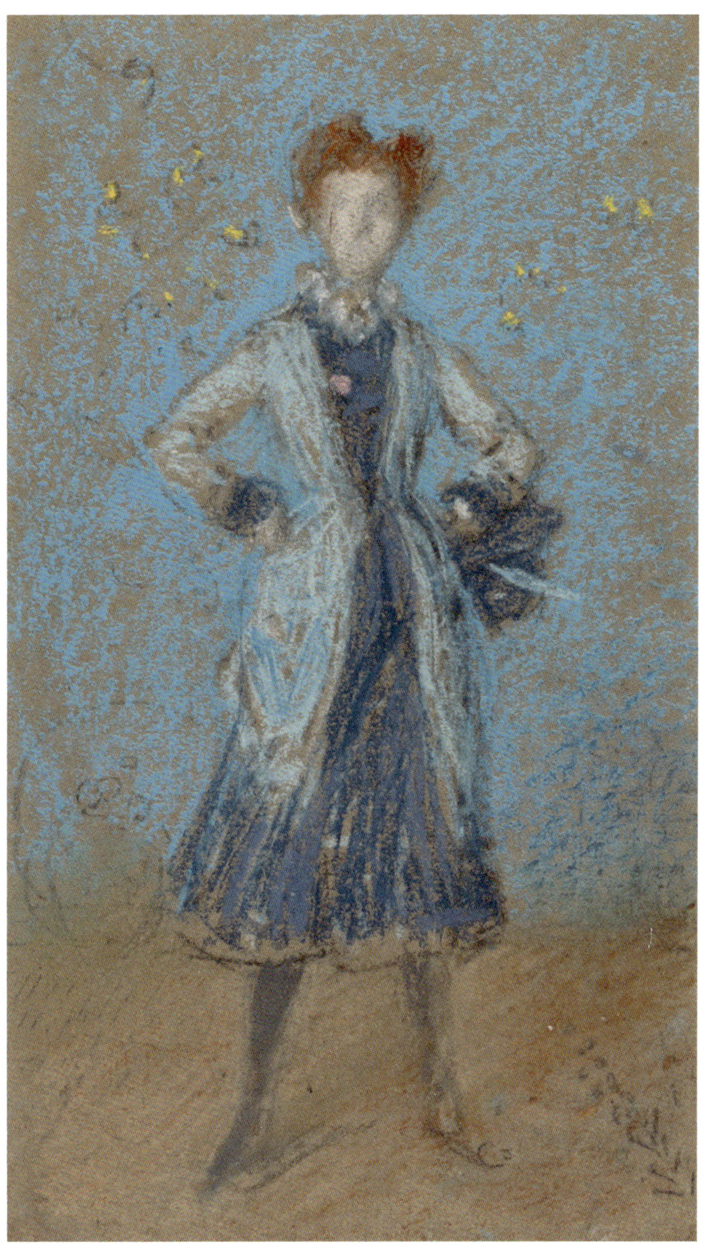

the point again as well as trumpet his allegiance to Van Dyck through deploying Van Dyckian methods as well as dress. Indeed, the year after Reynolds had delivered his *Seventh Discourse*, Gainsborough caused a sensation at the Royal Academy with *The Hon. Mrs Graham* (fig. 11), the first time he had exhibited there in five years. The painting itself had been finished in 1775, just before *The Hon. Frances Duncombe* (fig. 26) where the same extraordinary blue colour features in the equally remarkable 'Van Dyck' dress.[54]

Gainsborough was by no means the only artist to have had an ambivalent, sometimes fractious relationship with the Academy and its first president. But this enduring myth of *The Blue Boy*, often repeated in reviews and catalogues, has relevance beyond the painter's lifetime, not least in affirming artistic independence and innovation in contradiction to received wisdom. By the nineteenth century, appreciation for Gainsborough's masterpiece had become in part nostalgic, a perception that this bucolic image of youth and beauty represented a vanished world, prior to industrialisation, urbanisation and ensuing uncertainty and instability.[55] And bearing in mind the growing fame of *The Blue Boy*, it seems inevitable that other admired child portraits, such as Lawrence's '*Pinkie*' and '*The Red Boy*', should have become known by similarly colour-coded sobriquets (fig. 39; cat. 7).

However, *The Blue Boy* could equally act as a pointer to a variety of artistic concerns and innovations, as time and taste moved on. The maverick American artist James McNeill Whistler, who was often at odds with the art establishment and even published a book entitled *The Gentle Art of Making Enemies* (1890), may have seen something in *The Blue Boy* that chimed with his own attitude and circumstance, beyond being a spur to his ambitions as a society portrait painter (see the essay by Susanna Avery-Quash and Jacqueline Riding in this book). Indeed, among Whistler's pioneering arrangements of colours in harmony, we find a series of studies and paintings of youthful sitters, dominated by a vibrant blue. And he gave each the same title, *The Blue Girl* (fig. 12).[56]

Fig. 11
Thomas Gainsborough (1727–1788)
The Hon. Mrs Graham, 1775–7
Oil on canvas, 237 × 154 cm
Scottish National Gallery

Fig. 12
James McNeill Whistler (1834–1903)
The Blue Girl: Portrait of Elinor Leyland, 1873–6
Pastel on brown paper, 25.2 × 14.5 cm
Freer Gallery of Art and Arthur M. Sackler Gallery, Washington. Gift of Charles Lang Freer (F1905.126a-c)

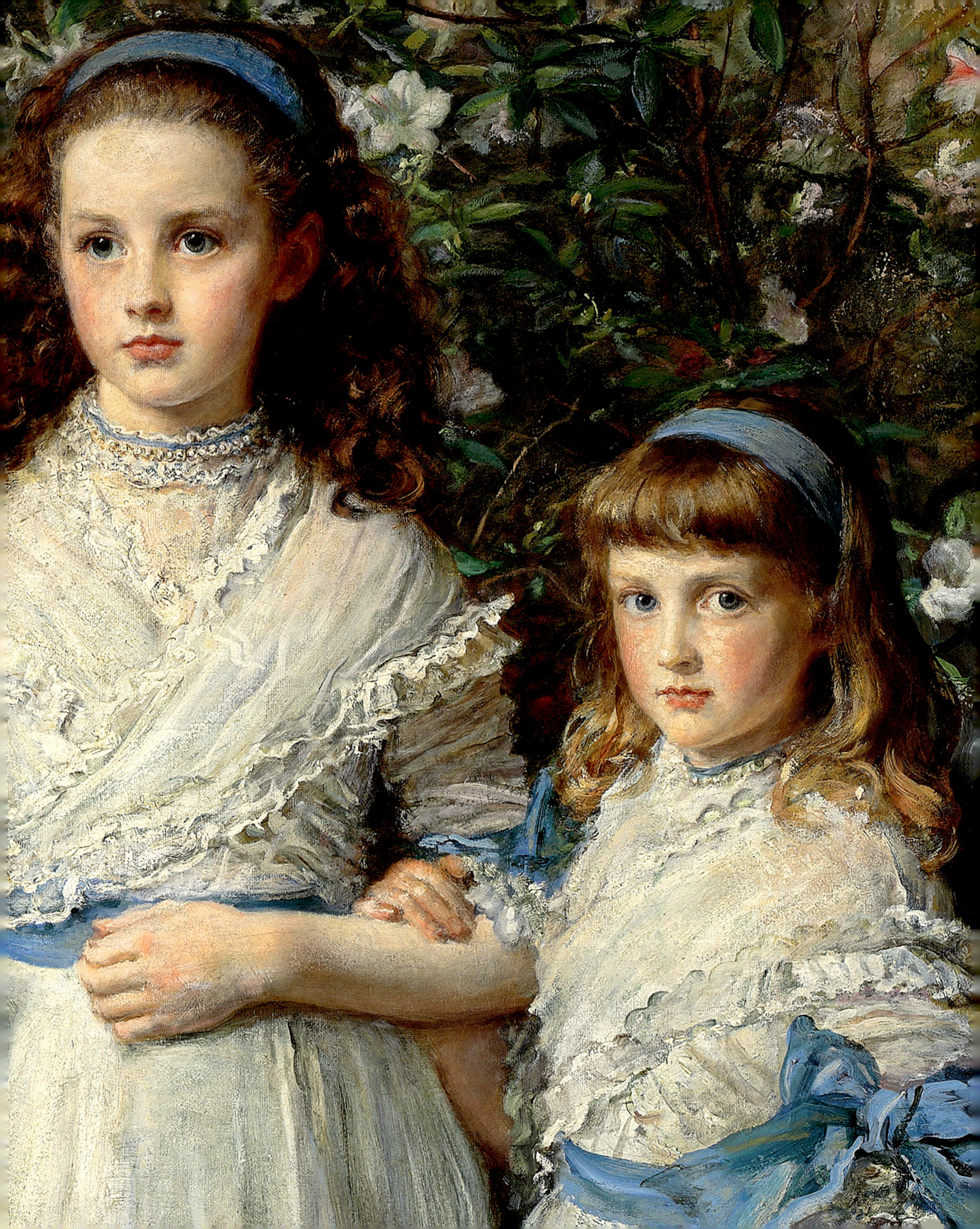

Gainsborough and the Status of British Art

Susanna Avery-Quash
and Jacqueline Riding

Detail of fig. 22

On 10 December 1788, Sir Joshua Reynolds PRA delivered his *Fourteenth Discourse* to the Royal Academy entitled 'CHARACTER OF GAINSBOROUGH: – HIS EXCELLENCIES AND DEFECTS'. Gainsborough's death only months before had presented an opportunity for such a survey, albeit one that was coloured by the often fractious personal and professional relationship between the two men – which had, in turn, caused a rift within the Academy. Crucially for Gainsborough's posthumous reputation, Reynolds used this forum to critique his former rival's artistic output and ideas in his own particular and partial terms. In so doing, Reynolds established the prism through which Gainsborough and his work would be viewed by commentators for decades – if not centuries – to come.

In the *Fourteenth Discourse*, Reynolds defines Gainsborough as a 'national' figure within the artistic establishment: 'If ever this nation should produce genius sufficient to acquire to us the honourable distinction of an English School, the name of Gainsborough will be transmitted to posterity, in the history of the Art, among the very first of that rising name.'[1] Furthermore, Reynolds presents Gainsborough as a worthy counterpoint to esteemed foreign painters of the past: 'I take more interest in and am more captivated with the powerful impression of nature which Gainsborough exhibited in his portraits and his landscapes, and the interesting simplicity and elegance of his little ordinary beggar-children, than with any of the works of that [the Roman] school since the time of Andrea Sacchi.'[2] Importantly, Reynolds also suggests that Gainsborough did not care to study exemplars of the past, a core principle espoused by the Royal Academy, following the lead of long-established European art academies. This was demonstrably untrue, for among Gainsborough's most obvious old master influences are several which he himself copied, namely Anthony van Dyck's *Lord John Stuart and his Brother, Lord Bernard Stuart* (fig. 5) and Titian's *Vendramin Family* (about 1540–5, National Gallery, London). Nor did Reynolds mention what others had reported as Gainsborough's dying words to him, perhaps because they did not fit comfortably with his characterisation of the deceased painter: 'We are all going to heaven, and Vandyke [sic] is of the company.'[3]

A leitmotif throughout the *Fourteenth Discourse* is that Gainsborough was an artist more attuned to the benefits of 'nature' over 'nurture'. To quote Reynolds again: 'It must be acknowledged that he saw [nature] with the eye of a painter; and gave faithful, if not poetical, representation of what he had before him.'[4] More specifically, Reynolds

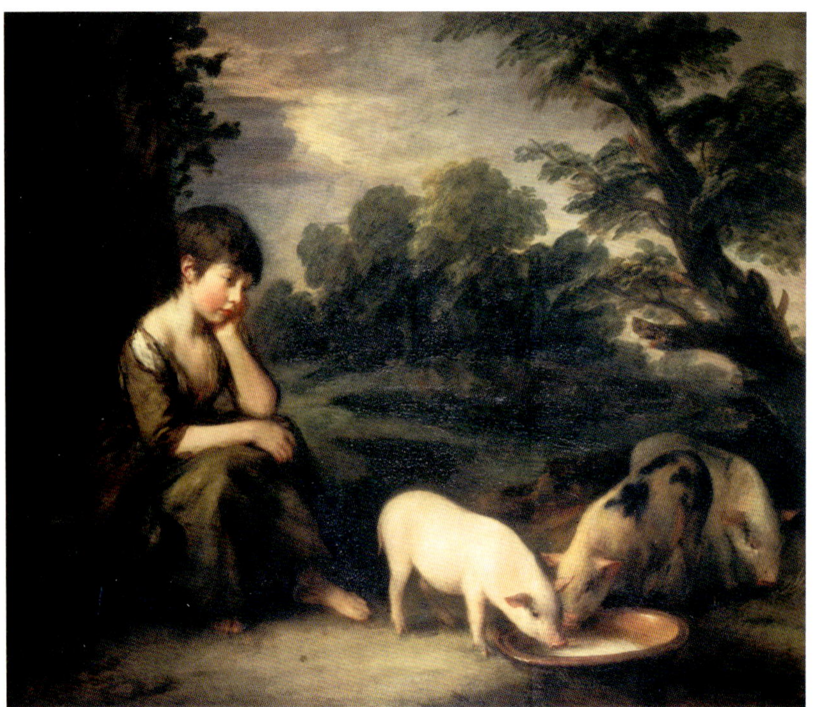

Fig. 13
Thomas Gainsborough (1727–1788)
Girl with Pigs, 1782
Oil on canvas, 125.7 × 148.6 cm
Private collection

considered Gainsborough's portraits as embodying the 'exact truth of resemblance', and his landscapes as offering a 'portrait-like representation of nature'. Reynolds owned a single work by Gainsborough, *Girl with Pigs* (fig. 13), a picture influenced by the seventeenth-century Spanish painter Murillo, a fact that only serves to underscore Reynolds's slanted reading of Gainsborough's work.

The Reynoldsian definition of Gainsborough as 'national' and 'natural' endured. For instance, in Alan Cunningham's *Lives of the Most Eminent British Painters* (1828), a pioneering British response to Giorgio Vasari's sixteenth-century biographies of fellow Italian artists, the author asserts that Gainsborough's 'paintings have a national look'.[5] Cunningham's *Lives* is important in embedding the idea that Britain had a school of painting that could stand its ground against the long-established Continental schools in Italy, the Netherlands and France. This notion had gained currency in the wake of Great Britain and her allies' victory over Napoleon Bonaparte in 1815 and then through the international acclaim that John Constable's *The Hay Wain* and *The Cornfield* (1821 and 1826, both National Gallery, London) and Thomas Lawrence's *Portrait of Charles William Lambton ('The Red Boy')* (cat. 7) received during their exhibition at the so-called 'British' Salons in Paris in 1824 and 1826/7. French commentators at the time regularly defined the British School in terms of 'real and natural poetry'.[6] Such a view of Gainsborough even crossed the Atlantic. As one example, the influential art critic John Ruskin's characterisation of Gainsborough as 'pure in his English feeling, profound in his seriousness, graceful in his gaiety' was footnoted in Edward Gilpin Johnson's edition of Reynolds's *Discourses*, published in Chicago, in 1891.[7]

The commercial promotion of British art was one way of refreshing a market saturated with Continental painting of the past, displaced from Italy, Spain, the Netherlands and France as a result of the recent wars. For instance, *The Blue Boy* (cat. 1) was puffed at the Peter Coxe, Burrell and Foster auction of 1802 as an 'incomparable Performance', which established Gainsborough 'among the First Class of Painters, both Antient [sic] and Modern'. The portrait was praised as having 'the Grace and Elegance of Van Dyck in the Figure, with a Countenance as forcibly expressed and rich as Morillio [sic], with the Management of Titian'.[8] Interestingly, John Hoppner, an established portrait painter, was the successful bidder; he doubtless acquired the work partly as a useful exemplar.[9]

The Blue Boy's reputation was secured to a large degree through its increasing visibility at public exhibitions. The Grosvenor family, who owned the painting from 1809 to 1921, lent it to many of the most significant exhibitions in Britain during the nineteenth century. On two occasions it was displayed at the British Institution, a private society founded in 1805, which mounted annual exhibitions until 1869 in Pall Mall.[10] Initially, the work of living British artists was prioritised there, but soon the work of esteemed deceased masters of all schools also featured. The British Institution exhibition of 1813 was a monographic show of Reynolds's work, while the following year, the focus was on other pillars of the British School, notably its 'father' William Hogarth, alongside three founding members of the Royal Academy including Gainsborough. *The Blue Boy* was one of the exhibits, as it was again in 1834, on which latter occasion, following the tradition of retaining certain works for students in an associated drawing school, it was kept back for study purposes. Its popularity is clear from the anecdote that by the end of the term, one whole wall was covered in copies.[11] The American painter James McNeill Whistler underscored the importance of Gainsborough's portraits in artistic circles in a letter to fellow artist Henri Fantin-Latour exhorting him to 'Come and see the [British Institution] exhibition – the Gainsboroughs and our *old loves*.'[12]

The role of organising annual old master exhibitions in London was assumed by the Royal Academy in 1870. Thereafter, a programme of winter exhibitions of European and British historic art counterbalanced the Academy's well-established practice of showing contemporary art each summer (indeed *The Blue Boy*'s debut had been at the Royal Academy in 1770). By juxtaposing the historic British School with its Continental counterparts, a 'battle of the schools' – reminiscent of Hogarth's satirical etching of 'The Battle of the Pictures' (1745), in which old master paintings gathered outside an auction house are shown attacking pictures by Hogarth as they emerge from his studio – was encouraged within and beyond the Academy. In the inaugural Royal Academy old master show, *The Blue Boy*, along with a Reynolds, was judged according to one critic to be more than a match for a neighbouring exhibit by the seventeenth-century French painter Claude Lorrain: 'Reynolds in *The Tragic Muse*, contributed by the Marquess of Westminster, and Gainsborough by *The Blue Boy*, exhibited at Manchester, assert for our native school a position, not only honourable, but singularly independent.'[13]

The critic was right to mention *The Blue Boy*'s presence at 'Manchester' – shorthand for the all-important 1857 Art Treasures exhibition at Old Trafford – when newly rich northern industrialists asserted their own cultural agency, challenging the dominance of the aristocracy and landed gentry, by organising the most ambitious display ever seen of national privately owned art. More than 1.25 million visitors encountered the 16,000 exhibits, which included hundreds of historic European paintings, such as Giovanni Bellini's *St Francis in the Desert* and Titian's *Rape of Europa*, as well as many examples of the British School. One area designated a 'British Portrait Gallery' was filled with 'a great number of Vandyck's, Holbein's, Kneller's,

Lely's, Reynolds's, Lawrence's, Gainsborough's, &c', displaying a range of portraits of private individuals alongside 'portraits of nearly all the King's [sic] and Queens of England, the most celebrated statesmen, generals, admirals, poets, painters, and dramatists':[14] thus consciously or not establishing the role of such exhibitions in celebrating national history as much as national art, discussed below. Although Gainsborough's portrait of Mrs Siddons (cat. 6) was praised, it was *The Blue Boy* that drew most attention, not least because it was given '[t]he place of honour ... the centre point of that long gallery [Salon D]', on account of the qualities of the portrait – 'the noble pose of the head – the frank, intelligent, and amiable face – the grace of attitude' and as 'a fortunate illustration of the style of Gainsborough as a painter, and of his character as a man'.[15] Although *The Blue Boy* was not lent to any of the three British seventeenth- and eighteenth-century and Romantic portraiture exhibitions at the South Kensington Museum in the 1860s, these shows were crucial in re-establishing reputations, developing a canon of British old masters, and promoting a sense of achievement and patriotic pride in the national school, from which the increasingly totemic painting could only benefit.

Between public exhibitions, *The Blue Boy*, as noted in the first surveys of British art collections of the 1840s by Anna Jameson and Gustav Waagen, could be viewed at Grosvenor House, which was among the most magnificent private art collections in the UK and one of the first to admit visitors.[16] Waagen saw *The Blue Boy* hanging in the drawing room facing Reynolds's portrait of Mrs Siddons, and thought it 'remarkable for animation and spirit'.[17] From the 1830s Grosvenor House reverted to being more private, largely because the National Gallery, opened in 1824, took up its mantle. Nonetheless, it still hosted private balls and semi-public charity events as well as numerous working men's groups, which meant that *The Blue Boy* retained its high profile.[18] Its visibility increased still further through being reproduced via numerous engravings and illustrations in books.[19]

As the nineteenth century progressed, the best place to study Gainsborough's art and compare it with the work of other British and foreign artists of the past and present was the National Gallery. Although no paintings by Gainsborough came with the foundation collections of John Julius Angerstein and George Beaumont in the early 1820s (these were dominated by Italian and French sixteenth- and seventeenth-century paintings, but did include a number of works by Van Dyck and Rubens, as well as Hogarth, Reynolds and David Wilkie), in 1826 Charles Long, a foundation trustee and director of the British Institution, presented *The Watering Place* (before 1777, National Gallery, London), explaining that he wanted the Gallery to include 'the Works of the most eminent Painters of the British School, and as there is no picture of one of our celebrated Artists [Gainsborough] in that Collection – I beg to present ... what I conceive to be one of the best Pictures of that Master'.[20] Four years later, Gainsborough's *The Market Cart* (1786, National Gallery, London) was presented by the British Institution, which had built up a nucleus of paintings for a future national collection.

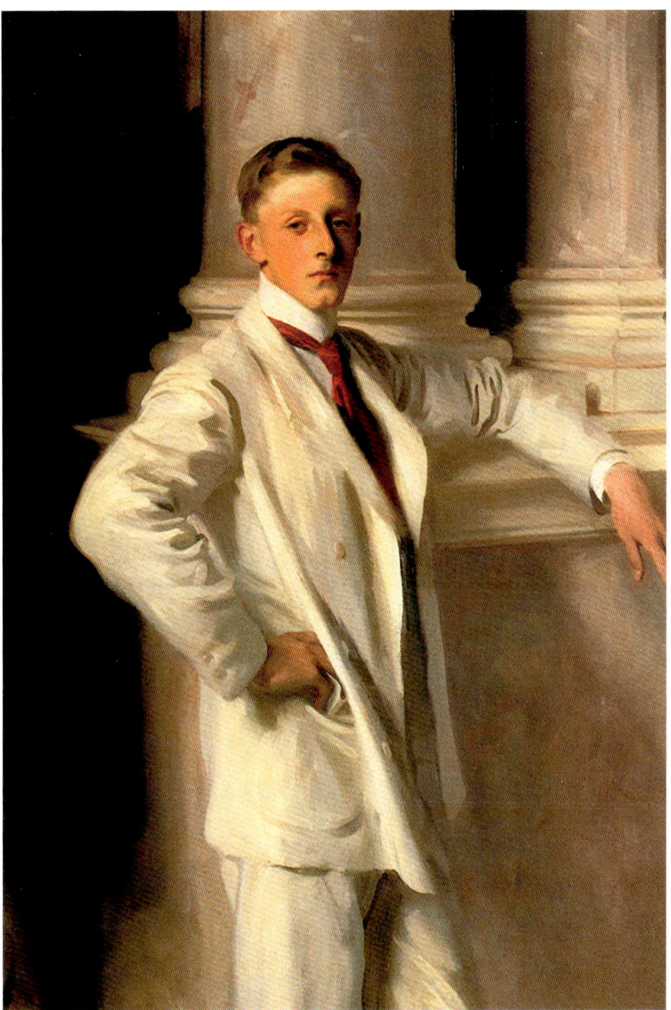

Fig. 14
John Singer Sargent (1856–1925)
Earl of Dalhousie, 1900
Oil on canvas, 152.4 × 101.6 cm
Private collection

It was Sir Charles Eastlake who, during his decade as inaugural director of the National Gallery from 1855, purchased the first portraits by Gainsborough, two of them in 1862, the same year that he also bought Reynolds's *Captain Robert Orme*. One was *Dr Ralph Schomberg*, painted in 1770, the same year as *The Blue Boy*.[21] A critic in *Blackwood's Magazine*, while dismissing *The Watering Place* as 'a dingy ditch', noted: 'the portrait of Ralph Schomberg ... redeems poor Gainsborough's fame. Gainsborough's forte was portrait, in that he stands almost unrivalled among those of his day, and in that walk he is original. He is more natural than Sir Joshua.'[22] Eastlake also purchased Gainsborough's *Mrs Siddons* (cat. 6), whose bright colouring and spirited handling demonstrate affinities with *The Blue Boy*, explaining why critics thought Gainsborough's painterly approach was 'natural' when compared to Reynolds's more studied, academic style.

With the opening of the Tate Gallery of British Art in 1897, a division of the British collection took place, with 'masterpieces' being retained at Trafalgar Square. The Curzon Report of 1915 explained to some extent the thinking behind this allocation: 'In Trafalgar Square will always be visible the supreme glories of British painting, alongside of their fellows, but to Millbank the student will go who desires to follow the history and evolution of indigenous art.'[23] That British portraiture predominated at Trafalgar Square bears witness to the genre's high standing at that time and the fact that it could be woven comparatively easily into a wider narrative of the development of European painting which included, among others, Titian, Rubens and Van Dyck. By contrast, many landscapes, an artistic genre in which the British School was recognised internationally to have excelled, were transferred to the Tate Gallery.[24] Gainsborough's *Market Cart* was one such; it returned to Trafalgar Square only in 1938.

British portraiture was embedded ever more deeply within the western European canon during the early decades of the twentieth century, when the National and Tate galleries accessioned a number of star-quality later nineteenth- and twentieth-century portraits, which were clearly inspired as much by British portraiture as by earlier Continental works. American painter John Singer Sargent's *Lord Ribblesdale* (1902, National Gallery, London), presented by the sitter in 1916, is a case in point, as are Whistler's monochromatic studies including *Symphony in White, No. 2: The Little White Girl* (1864), given in 1919 but later transferred to the Tate Gallery. Whistler went so far as to adopt Gainsborough's use of two-metre-long brushes, very liquid paint and 'odd scratches and marks',[25] and instigated a series of studies

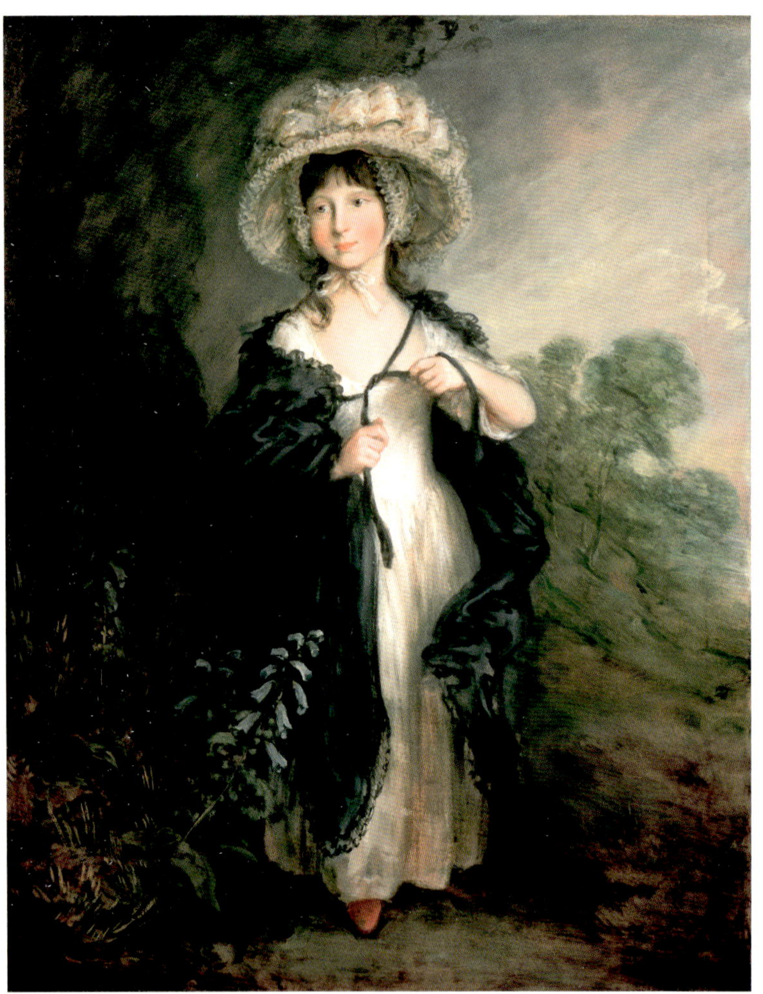

Fig. 15
Thomas Gainsborough (1727–1788)
Miss Elizabeth Haverfield,
early 1780s
Oil on canvas, 126.2 × 101 cm
The Wallace Collection, London

(fig. 12) and a large-scale oil painting of Elinor Leyland that are a clear riff on Gainsborough's boy in blue of a century earlier.[26] Here, in particular, the artist was said to have been interested in the 'blue cashmere and velvet' clothing which the painter described as an 'arrangement in blue', while Whistler's biographer, Thomas Robert Way, believed 'from certain remarks he made to me, that Gainsborough's "Blue Boy" was in his mind when he determined to attack this very difficult problem' (see Christine Riding's essay in this book.)[27]

While the National Gallery was acquiring and displaying British portraits of the type just noted – and thereby helping to create national icons – the wealthiest UK private collectors were likewise purchasing similar historic examples, whether by eighteenth-century British painters or earlier Continental masters. The 4th Marquess of Hertford added to the Gainsboroughs already in the Hertford collection, such as *Mrs Mary Robinson (Perdita)* bought by the 2nd Marquess in 1818, through the acquisition of numerous other full-length portraits including *Miss Elizabeth Haverfield* (fig. 15), a charming evocation of childhood, acquired in 1859. Unsurprisingly, given the by now universal popularity of *The Blue Boy*, those works that made reference to Gainsborough's masterpiece were among the most expensive and prized. A prime instance is Gainsborough's own *Lord Archibald Hamilton*,[28] a signed head-and-shoulders roundel in blue Van Dyck attire, for which another wealthy British collector, Ferdinand de Rothschild, paid £4,410, a sum nearly four times that paid for the companion painting depicting the elder brother in a less appealing black suit. Ferdinand's sister, Alice de Rothschild, later purchased as suitable pendants to her brother's acquisitions Gainsborough's portrait of Master Francis Nicholls, whose pink silk Van Dyck costume later earned it the nickname '*The Pink Boy*' (fig. 18), at the time that *The Blue Boy* was making its mark at the 1857 Art Treasures exhibition, and Joseph Highmore's earlier half-length portrait of a boy wearing a mustard-yellow Van Dyck costume (1748).[29]

It was on collections like Waddesdon Manor and Hertford House that certain American plutocrats later modelled their own London homes and art collections, the latter of which, for tax reasons, were kept in London. For instance, John Pierpont Morgan's London residence at Prince's Gate had a dining room whose walls dazzled with full-length portraits by Reynolds, Gainsborough and Romney. Unsurprisingly,

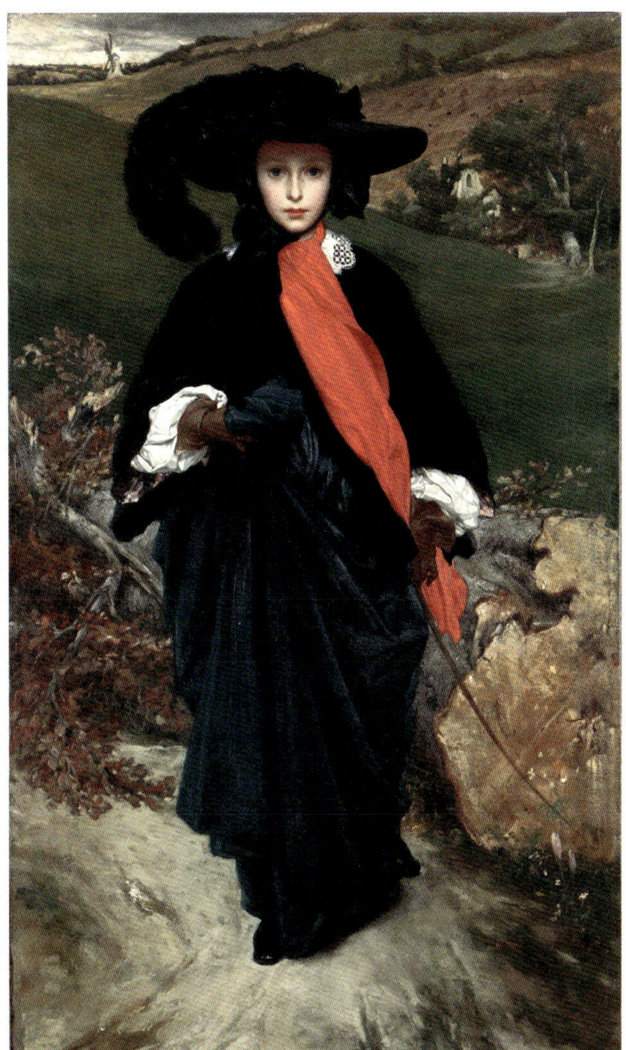

some of the important paintings which eventually found their way to the United States came from these British private collections: Henry E. Huntington, for example, purchased three pictures formerly in the Rothschild Collection, through Joseph Duveen.[30]

Nineteenth-century art patrons, first British and later American, also continued the tradition of commissioning portraits. As Richard Ormond has argued, it was the most avant-garde artists – starting with George Frederic Watts, then John Everett Millais and Whistler, and later Sargent – who revivified portraiture in Britain by consciously positioning themselves as the heirs to what was an increasingly revered and lucrative British tradition that stretched back to Reynolds, Gainsborough and before them, via Hogarth and Sir Godfrey Kneller, to Sir Peter Lely and Van Dyck.[31] For instance, Leighton's *Portrait of May Sartoris*, a soulful, poetic image of a young girl in a black riding habit slashed with red, painted against a view of the English countryside (fig. 16), melds Van Dyck with the pose and frank expression of *The Blue Boy*, while Millais's portrait of Anthony de Rothschild (1891, Ascott House, Bedfordshire) represents a far less subtle evocation of Gainsborough's famous painting. Sargent's dynastic portrait, *The Marlborough Family* (fig. 17) with the 'heir and the spare' in Van Dyck attire, acted as a resonant pendant to a portrait of the 4th Duke's family painted by Reynolds of 1778. Arguably, Sargent was closer to Gainsborough in artistic temperament, as can be seen in his *Earl of Dalhousie* (fig. 14), which, in its economy and allusiveness manages to conjure up both the swagger of Van Dyck's *Stuart Brothers* (cat. 4) and Gainsborough's confident boy in blue. Notably, *The Marlborough Family* (fig. 17) included the 9th Duke of Marlborough's American wife, Consuelo Vanderbilt, and it was the newly rich and socially ambitious Americans who adopted many of the customs of the landed families into which they were marrying or which they were gradually supplanting. As well as acquiring titles, they lived and entertained in a grand style and with conspicuous expenditure decorated their newly acquired country seats and London houses with portraits old and new.

In the same spirit of emulation were the Van Dyckian costumes worn at fashionable masquerade balls, events which occurred throughout the nineteenth century in Britain, and were then imitated in the United States. Among the grandest were the mid-century royal costume balls at Buckingham Palace including the 'Stuart Ball' of 1851, which evoked the reign of Charles II (fig. 19), and later the Devonshire House Fancy Dress Ball of 1897. Extant photographs of the latter occasion reveal that many of the guests used family portraits as guides, including the Hon. Mrs Baillie, whose costume mimicked

Fig. 16
Frederic Leighton (1830–1896)
Portrait of May Sartoris, about 1860
Oil on canvas, 152.1 × 90.2 cm
Kimbell Art Museum, Fort Worth

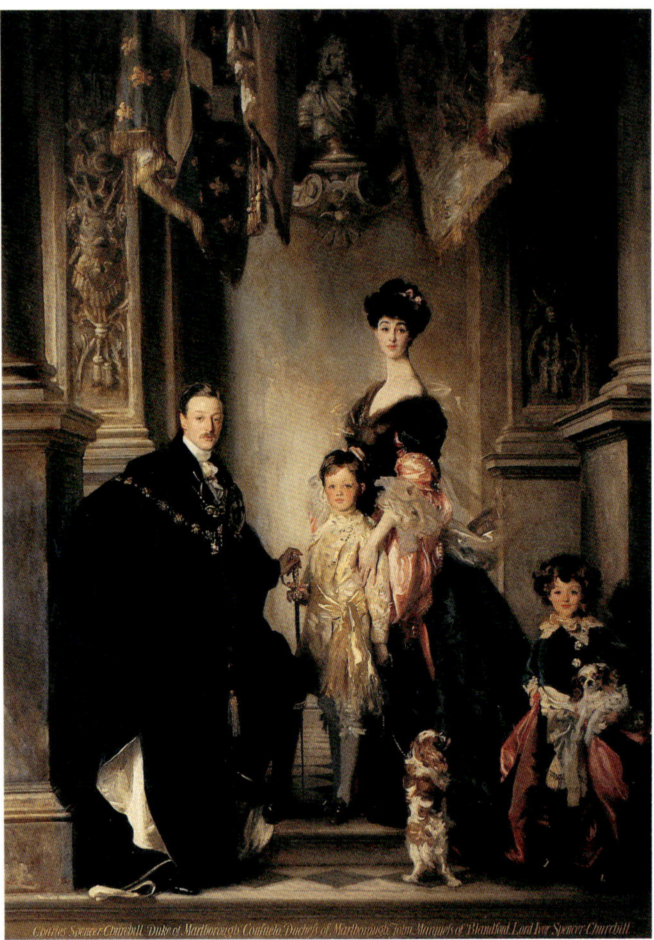

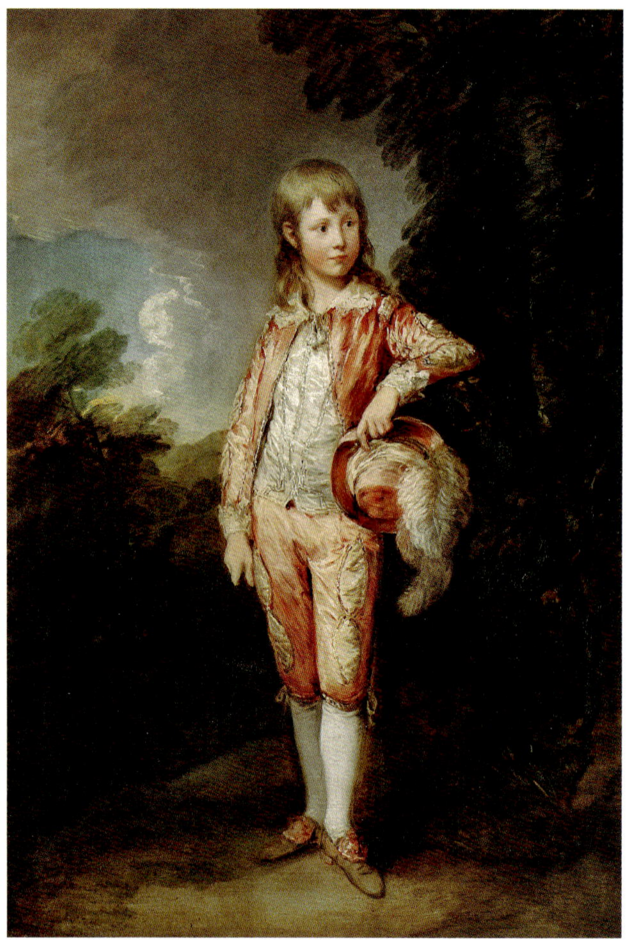

Fig. 17
John Singer Sargent (1856–1925)
The Marlborough Family, 1904–5
Oil on canvas, 287 × 238.7 cm
Duke of Marlborough collection

Fig. 18
Thomas Gainsborough (1727–1788)
Francis Nicholls 'The Pink Boy', 1782
Oil on canvas, 167.6 x 116.8cm
Waddesdon (The National Trust) Bequest of James de Rothschild, 1957

that worn by the unusually named Colin Campbell in Gainsborough's *Baillie Family*, and Isabella, Countess Howe, whose costume was taken from Gainsborough's *Mary, Countess Howe*.[32] In the United States, velvet suits with a lace collar, ultimately derived from Van Dyck's royal child portraiture and Gainsborough's *Blue Boy*, gained further popularity after the publication of Frances Hodgson Burnett's *Little Lord Fauntleroy* (1886), which was turned into a Broadway production two years later. Back in Britain, *The Blue Boy* – and associated offshoots like '*The Pink Boy*' (fig. 18) – and *Little Lord Fauntleroy* proved popular inspirations at the Juvenile Fancy Dress Ball held in Leeds on 12 January 1891 (fig. 20) with four 'Boy Blue' costumes, three Fauntleroys and even a 'Charles II' among the Bo-Peeps, Prince Charmings and goblins.[33]

Gainsborough's work also entered the popular consciousness through its adaptation in numerous nineteenth-century historical genre pictures. Importantly, the National Portrait Gallery had been established in 1856 during a period when professional portrait painting was widely perceived as in decline. Its demise was countered by the rise of subject or narrative paintings from the early 1800s, as popularised by Wilkie, and the market for contemporary and historical genre paintings of the next generation, as exemplified by the work of Edward Matthew Ward, William Powell Frith and Augustus Egg.

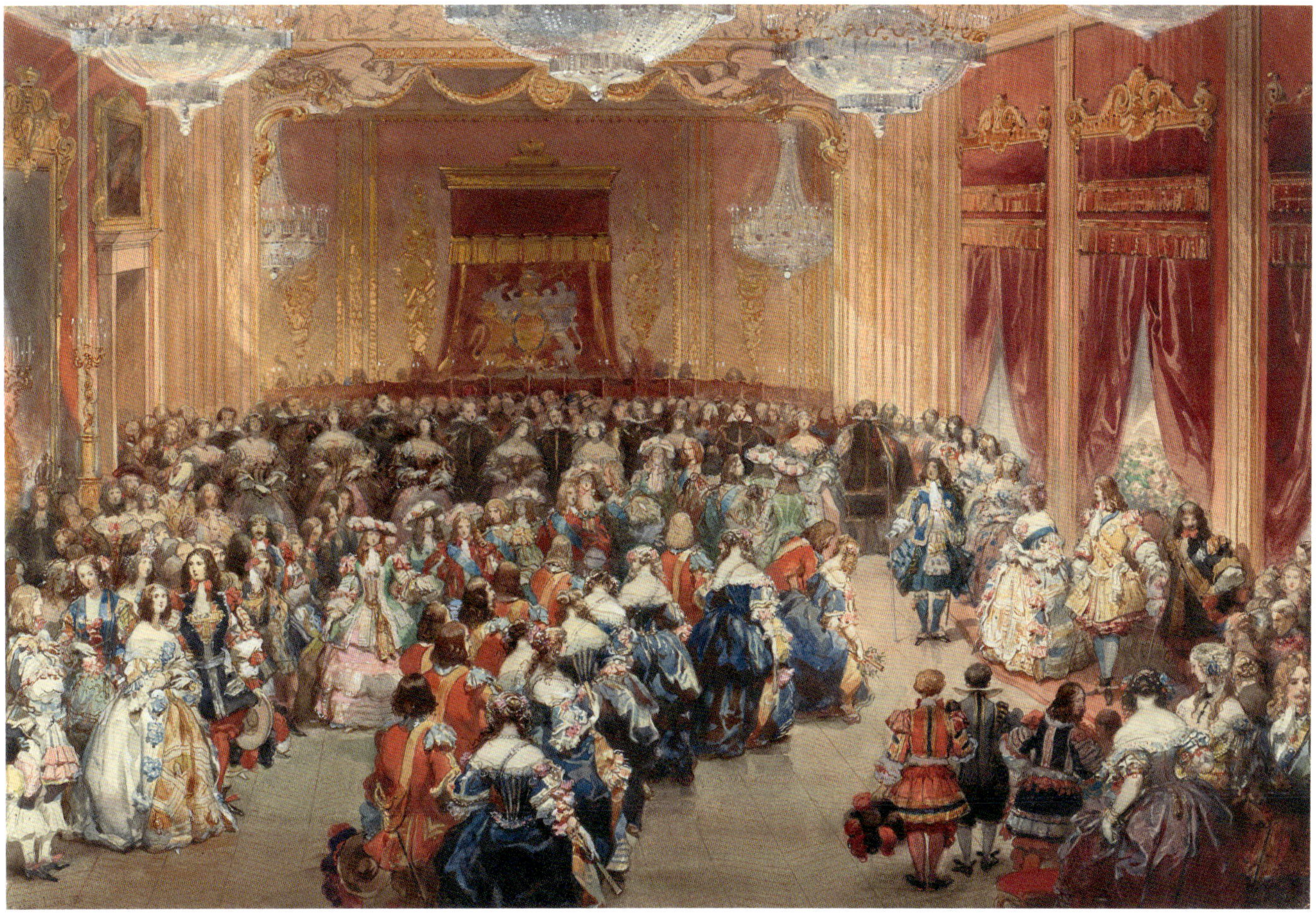

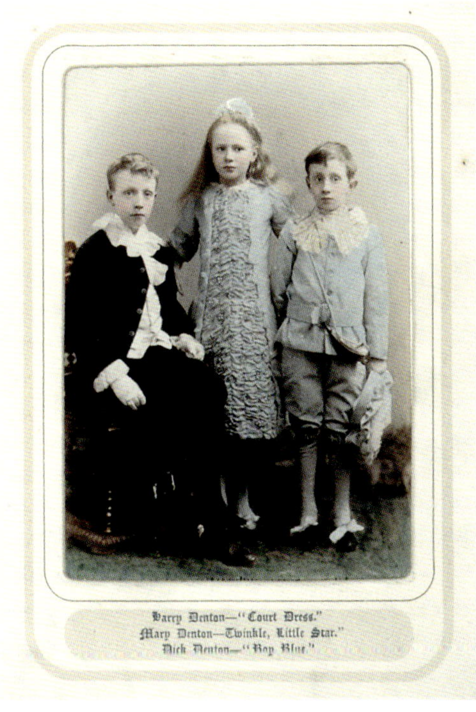

Fig. 19
Eugène Louis Lami (1800–1890)
The Stuart Ball at Buckingham Palace, 13 June 1851, 1851
Pencil, watercolour and bodycolour, 30.6 x 45.2 cm
The Royal Collection / HM Queen Elizabeth II

Fig. 20
Juvenile Fancy Dress Ball, Leeds,
12 January 1891
Photograph
Souvenir Album, Leeds Museum and Art Gallery

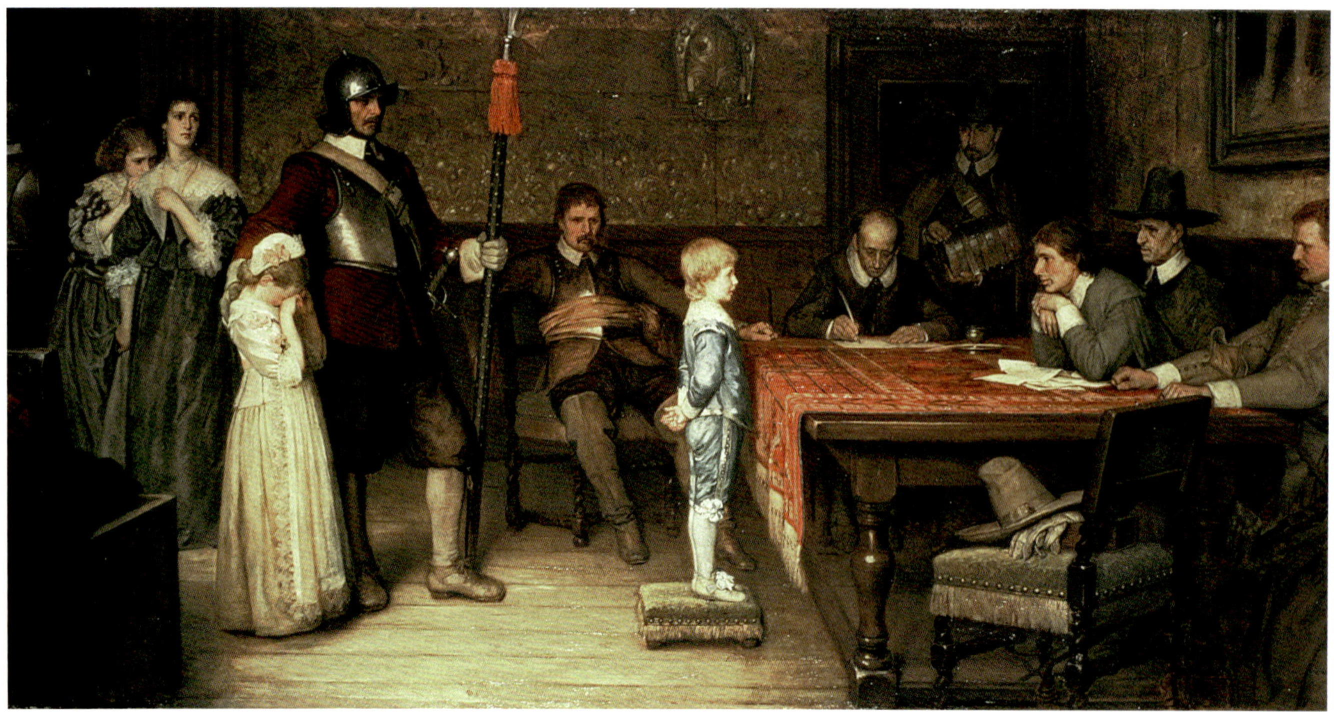

Fig. 21
William Frederick Yeames (1835–1918)
'And when did you last see your Father?', 1878
Oil on canvas, 131 × 251.5 cm
Walker Art Gallery, Liverpool. Purchased by the Walker Art Gallery in 1878

Indeed, throughout the Romantic period the depiction of history became more inclusive, featuring the lives of ordinary people as much as royalty and national heroes. The hugely influential historical novels of Sir Walter Scott presented the past as immediate and accessible, populated by characters with all the passions and sensibilities of their modern-day counterparts. Scott's first great success was *Waverley* (1814), set during the Jacobite Rebellion of 1745–6. A similar desire to reconcile the contested history of the Stuart dynasty can be seen in the murals executed for the new Palace of Westminster from the 1840s, which included a series focusing on the Civil War (1642–9), Interregnum (1649–60), and 'Glorious Revolution' (1688) – a choice guided by the historian Thomas Babington Macaulay, whose multi-volume *History of England* was published from 1848. While some murals, such as Charles West Cope's of the burial of Charles I, focused on leading players, other artists concentrated on everyday people caught up in the fray. Likewise, Millais's *The Proscribed Royalist, 1651* (1851, Lloyd-Webber Collection), exhibited at the Royal Academy in 1853, depicts a Puritan woman protecting a fleeing Royalist after Oliver Cromwell had defeated the future Charles II.

This significant reappraisal of British history brought characters representative of the past, including Van Dyckian figures, to life. A prime instance is William Frederick Yeames's *'And when did you last see your Father?'* (fig. 21, acquired in the same year by the Walker Art Gallery), which depicts the son of a Royalist being questioned by Parliamentarians during the English Civil War. While the boy is clearly based on *The Blue Boy*, Yeames's painting also demonstrates the importance of young people in this reimagining of history, many

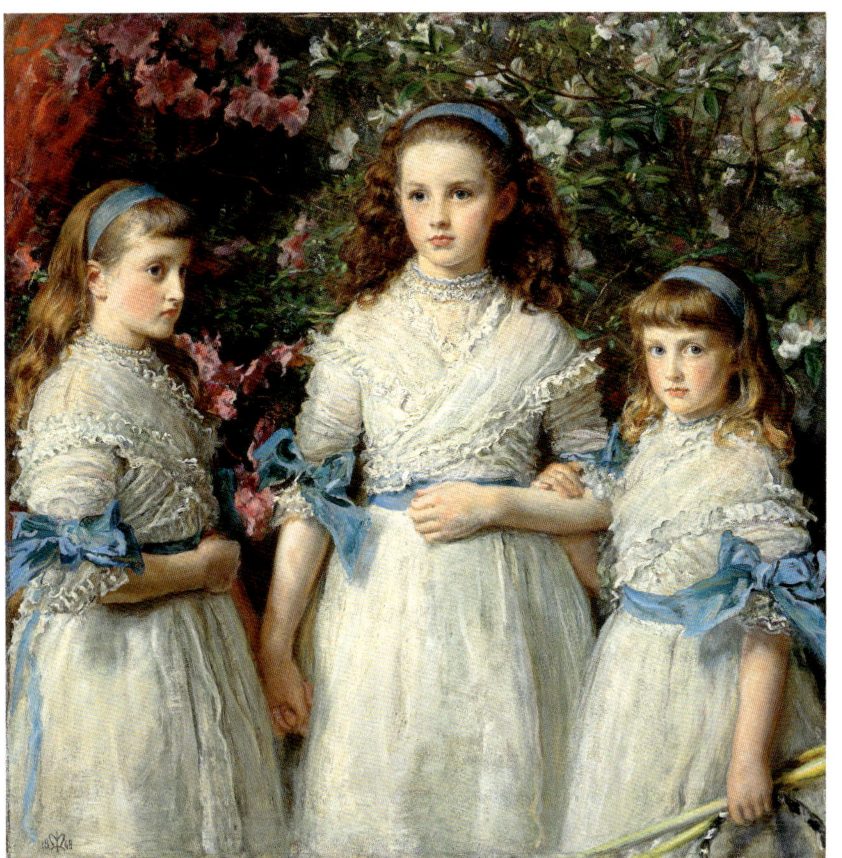

Fig. 22
John Everett Millais (1829–1896)
Sisters, 1868
Oil on canvas, 108 × 108 cm
Private collection

the victims of power, politics and civil war. Similarly, Millais painted both *The Princes in the Tower* and *Princess Elizabeth in the Prison at St James's* (1878 and 1879, both Royal Holloway, University of London). In these imaginary portraits as much as in his likenesses of real children such as *Nina Lehmann* (1868–9, private collection) and *Sisters* (fig. 22), the latter self-consciously based on Reynolds and Gainsborough and featuring his three daughters, Millais intentionally generalised the sitters, in order to explore ideas concerning the pathos of childhood and fleeting innocence, linked to a sense of loss, sadness or death.[34] Furthermore, through the works discussed here by Millais, Leighton, Whistler and others, it is clear that eighteenth-century British paintings such as *The Blue Boy* influenced the aesthetic movement in Britain, with its championship of beauty and 'art for art's sake'.

The 'rehabilitation' of the Stuart dynasty – synonymous with the civil-war turmoil of the seventeenth-century and then the Jacobite risings from 1689 to 1746 – could occur because it had been systematically neutralised as a political force from the 1760s. The 'Exhibition of the Royal House of Stuart' at The New Gallery, London in 1889, with Queen Victoria as patron and major lender, offered an unprecedented opportunity to view Stuart/Jacobite portraits and 'relics'. Although she represented the very dynasty that the later Stuarts had sought to replace (most famously, Charles Edward Stuart in 1745–6), Victoria by now viewed them as her tragic kin.[35] The doomed romantic allure of the Stuart dynasty – whether as depicted by Van Dyck himself or via his surrogate Gainsborough and *The Blue Boy* – coupled with the popularity of Scott's *Waverley* and historical genre/narrative paintings more broadly, combined to inspire John Pettie's *Bonnie Prince Charlie entering the Ballroom at Holyroodhouse* of 1891–2 (fig. 23). In a pose echoing *The Blue Boy* and with the insolence of Van Dyck's *Stuart Brothers* (cat. 4), the 'bonnie prince' symbolises a cause in ruins, its youth doomed. The highly emotive theme of 'lost youth' would reach its apogee with the First World War, a significant factor in the British reaction to the sale of *The Blue Boy* within a few years of the conflict ending.

If *The Blue Boy* had become so popular in Britain, why was Henry Huntington able to purchase it in October 1921 and export it in January 1922? The irony of this period is that while members of the British nobility, such as Lord Ribblesdale, were patronising the likes of Sargent as a way of reasserting their influence over that most 'aristocratic', and now British, of art forms, the grand manner portrait, so many such paintings were being sold. The key factor was price. *The Blue Boy* was sold for a princely $728,000 (£182,000, now nearly £9 million), the highest price which had ever been paid for a painting, and no-one in Britain, whether an individual or an institution, had sufficient means to compete. On the one hand, the British aristocracy and landed gentry had been selling off artistic assets to raise funds in the wake of the agricultural crisis of the 1870s, increased taxation through the introduction of death duty in 1894 and the so-called 'People's Budget' of 1909. On the other hand, affluent American buyers found themselves ideally placed to take advantage given that the United States' economy was booming and in 1909 the 20 per cent import tariff on works of art over a century old was scrapped. British dealers stepped in and were adept at stirring up rivalry between premier US-based clients for the newly available eighteenth-century British portraits. Joseph Duveen, who sold *The Blue Boy* to Huntington, was the dealer who did most to inflate such prices, an early instance taking place in 1901, when he paid £14,050 for John Hoppner's *Lady Louisa Manners*, the highest price achieved at a British auction for a painting until that date.

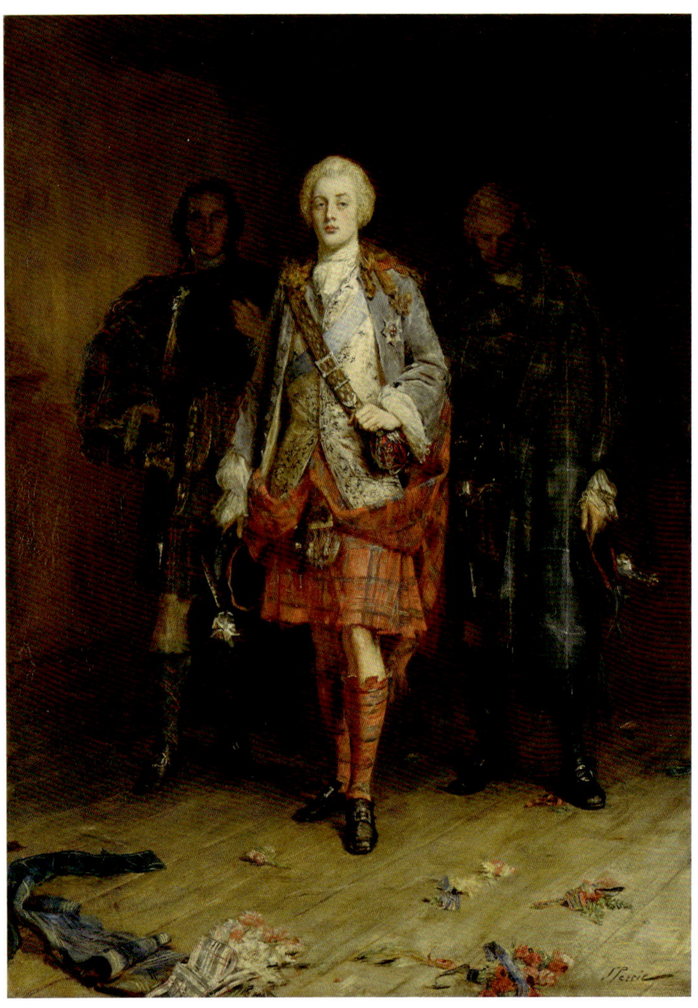

Fig. 23
John Pettie (1839–1893)
Bonnie Prince Charlie entering the Ballroom at Holyroodhouse, 1891–2
Oil on canvas, 158.8 × 114.3 cm
The Royal Collection / HM Queen Elizabeth II

In the face of such escalating prices, even the UK's National Art Collections Fund, established in 1903 to prevent masterpieces from leaving British shores, was ineffective. In fact, it had already assisted the National Gallery to save Velázquez's *Rokeby Venus* in 1906 (purchased for £45,000) and Hans Holbein's full-length portrait of Christina of Denmark in 1907 (£72,000),[36] the latter particularly contentious because, having been on loan at the National Gallery from the Dukes of Norfolk for many years, it was generally considered as already belonging to the national collection. But those earlier financial outlays were nothing compared with the sum now in question concerning *The Blue Boy*, and despite appeals in the national press, there were insufficient finances to save the picture from export.

When *The Blue Boy* was put on display for three weeks at the National Gallery (fig. 24) ahead of its transatlantic departure, *The Times* reported that 90,000 visitors came to bid it farewell.[37] It stole the show despite the fact that it was displayed among 'a collection of English glories, Hogarth, Reynolds, Morland and all the constellation of the eighteenth century',[38] including Hogarth's *The Shrimp Girl*

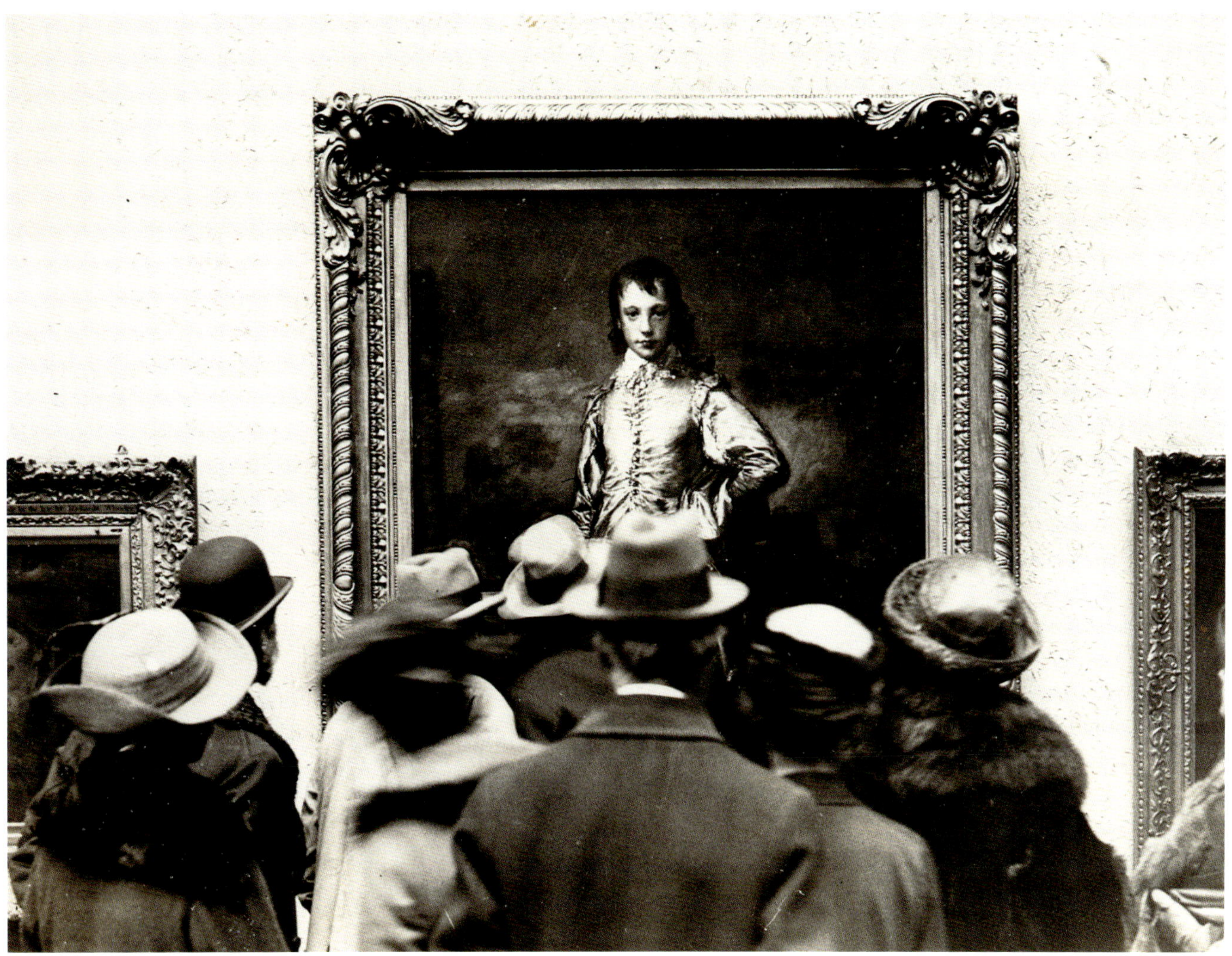

Fig. 24
The Blue Boy on display at the National Gallery, London, 1922

(about 1740–5, National Gallery, London) and *Mrs Salter* (1741, now Tate, London), Reynolds's 'The Three Graces' (*Three Ladies adorning a Term of Hymen*, 1773, now Tate, London) and Gainsborough's own portrait of *Mrs Siddons* (cat. 6). On the last day, '[a]ll day long luxurious cars were driving up to the National Gallery, and in Gallery XXV, there was a crowd four or five deep gazing reverentially at the dazzling sapphire blue of the Boy's suit.'[39]

The public upset caused by the sale of *The Blue Boy* mirrored in many ways the plotline of Henry James's last novel, *The Outcry* (1911), which revolved around the contemporary issue of the buying up of Britain's artistic treasures by rich Americans. However, the major difference was that the fiction had a 'happy ever after' ending: an English aristocrat, Lord Theign, not only thwarts American millionaire Beckenridge Bender by refusing to sell him a prized Reynolds portrait, but also gives another work to the National Gallery. By contrast, in the real-life case of Gainsborough's portrait a decade later, a private American millionaire, of the kind foiled in James's novel, did become *The Blue Boy*'s delighted new owner.

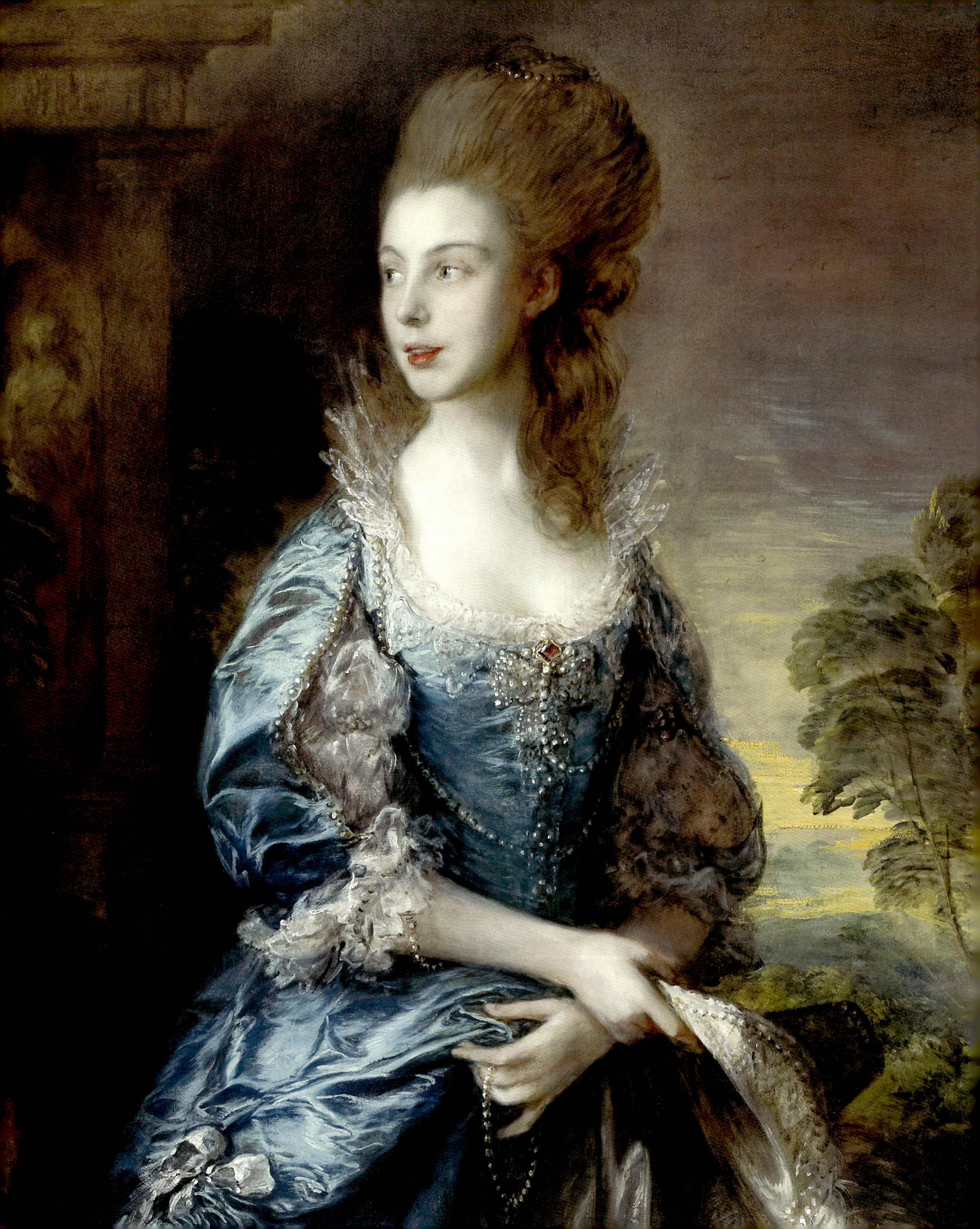

Testament of Youth

Melinda McCurdy

On 10 October 1921 the *Chicago Herald-Examiner* reported that renowned art dealer Joseph Duveen had acquired *The Blue Boy* from its owner, the Duke of Westminster, after lengthy negotiations. According to the newspaper, Duveen intended to take the painting to New York the following January, where it would be 'open for purchase by the highest bidder'.[1] It was further reported that the painting, which was currently housed in the 'basement' of the National Gallery, having been taken there for safety during the First World War (1914–18), had been purchased 'for no one except the house of Duveen'. Although it was printed that Duveen had made the announcement that very day, the information was patently false. American businessman Henry E. Huntington had written from Chateau Beauregard, the villa he and his wife had leased near Paris, to the Duveen firm three days previously, 'to confirm the conversation I had with your Sir Joseph Duveen today, whereby I agree to purchase from you the picture by Thomas Gainsborough known as "The Blue Boy"'.[2] Duveen's statement to the newspaper that *The Blue Boy* was to be sold in New York was certainly intended to generate publicity for the sale, and by extension the Duveen firm. However, in naming the painting's new home, Duveen also acknowledged the rising cultural, economic and political status of the United States. Although it had long been an icon of British art, *The Blue Boy* would soon be embraced by an America beginning its transformation into a global power.

The Chicago article was among the first to report that *The Blue Boy* would be exhibited in London before being shipped to America. By 14 December Duveen had arranged with Sir Charles Holmes, the director of the National Gallery, to place the painting on public view there. On 3 January 1922 the art dealer reported to Huntington that *The Blue Boy* was 'beautifully hung' with two other works by Gainsborough in the National Gallery collection, his portrait of *Mrs Siddons* (cat. 6) and the unfinished oil sketch of the artist's daughters (fig. 37). The grouping was perhaps more significant than anyone at the time realised. It seems that *The Blue Boy* may have been on display near his own cousins, if, as recent scholarship has suggested, the figure's model was Gainsborough's nephew and studio assistant, Gainsborough Dupont.[3] Henry Huntington had also purchased Sir Joshua Reynolds's own portrait of the actress, *Sarah Siddons as the Tragic Muse* (fig. 38), from the Westminster collection in November and it, too, was about to leave for America.

Detail of fig. 26

By the time of its exhibition at the National Gallery, *The Blue Boy*'s familiarity among British audiences ran so deep it could nearly be described in terms of a personal, or even familial, relationship. In addition to the painting's noteworthy accessibility, described in the second essay of this volume, the image of the boy in blue had also made its way into people's homes through publications, prints and ceramic figurines, such as those produced around 1900 for W.P. & G. Phillips of London in imitation of eighteenth-century Chelsea ware.[4] Parodies and popular stage productions that referenced the costumed figure, often conflated with the nursery-rhyme character 'Little Boy Blue', as in the 1876 pantomime *Little Goody Two Shoes or Harlequin Blue Boy*, or the title character in Frances Hodgson Burnett's theatrical adaptation of her novel *Little Lord Fauntleroy*, ensured it was part of Britain's collective consciousness.[5] When it became clear that *The Blue Boy* had been sold to an American, many responded as if the nation were losing one of its own sons. An article titled 'A Farewell', published in *The Times* on 27 January, two days after the exhibition's close, described the emotional response to the painting's departure:

> Absurdly enough, perhaps, one or two of us had tears in our eyes, we hardly knew why. Perhaps it was because some of the lovely youth of our country seemed to be going with him, some of the grace of the old time, when men and women wore those gorgeous clothes, and were untroubled by the many self-questionings of our generations; something of the courtly grace and serene carriage of a people who knew themselves a great people and were not ashamed to own it.[6]

Only a handful of years before the sale of *The Blue Boy*, Britain had experienced the real loss of what the painting had come to symbolise by the early 1920s. The devastation brought about by the First World War is difficult to fathom. More than 700,000 British military personnel were killed or missing in action, while nearly two million more returned home wounded. The majority of these were young men, perhaps only a few years older than the boy in Gainsborough's painting. Its departure, one more loss, would have resonated deeply.[7] In addition to the many wounded encountered on the streets of every town, the erection of national memorials and the enactment of commemorative ceremonies were visible reminders of the war's devastation. A new stone Cenotaph, replacing an earlier temporary structure, had been recently unveiled on Whitehall, five minutes' walk from the National Gallery, during the ceremonial funeral of the Unknown British Warrior. Witnessed by tens of thousands, the event took place on 11 November 1920, nearly exactly one year before the sale of *The Blue Boy*. Other memorials map the horrors of war onto the bodies of young men, who, like *The Blue Boy*, became symbols of the nation's loss. The memorial at Paddington Station (unveiled in 1922) is just one of many examples (fig. 25). Here, the bronze figure of a young soldier stands against another cenotaph-like structure honouring the more than 25,000 workers of the Great Western Railway lost in

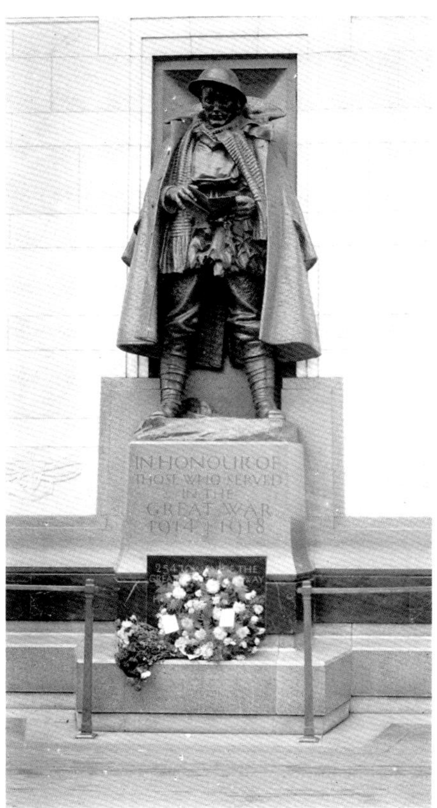

Fig. 25
Charles Sargeant Jagger (1885–1934)
Great Western Railway War Memorial,
Paddington Railway Station, London

the war. He waits on the platform, a letter clutched in his hands, his sunken eyes and hollow cheeks a testament to the conflict's toll. Among those who survived, the war caused more than just physical wounds. Many members of this 'lost generation', as American writers Gertrude Stein and Ernest Hemingway would term it, suffered ongoing mental trauma rooted in the experience of mass destruction, its aftermath dramatised in literature of the period as a mixture of hopelessness and hedonism. Vera Brittain eloquently described the impact of war on those at home in her autobiographical work *Testament of Youth* (1933), which recounts her struggle with grief over the deaths of young men she knew, including her brother, fiancé and friends. The association of portraits with national loss was not new. After the English Civil War, Anthony van Dyck's portraits of Charles I and the royal family served as symbols of political affiliation as well as reminders of the losses suffered by the Royalist cause.[8]

Van Dyck had revolutionised British portraiture during the reign of Charles I. The relaxed elegance of his portrait style was a world away from the more rigid and stately portraits of the Tudor and Jacobean courts, and the new naturalness it projected greatly impacted artists who came after him, in Britain and beyond. In the eighteenth century, Gainsborough, Reynolds and George Romney produced breezy full-lengths that presented an image of status all the more potent because it appeared effortless. The feeling of spontaneity Van Dyck created in his portraiture is perhaps even more pronounced in his images of children. Despite its obvious markers of royal status, his portrait of *The Five Eldest Children of Charles I* (fig. 2) presents the crown prince and his siblings as real children instead of miniature adults, as had been the norm. Princess Elizabeth, at right, looks fondly at her youngest sister, a baby who wiggles on her lap, while the future king Charles II stands proudly in the centre, barely taller than the giant mastiff on whose head he rests his hand. The painting left the royal collection in 1650, but had been reacquired by George III in 1765, just five years before Gainsborough exhibited *The Blue Boy*.[9] The later artist understood Van Dyck's ability to capture something of his sitters' humanity in their portraits. It was a quality for which he also strived. Contemporaries noted the psychological penetration that marks his work: 'He shows the face in more points of view than one, and by that means it strikes everyone who has seen the original with being a resemblance; that while the portrait with a rigid outline exhibits the countenance only in one disposition of mind, his gives it in many.'[10] Although *The Blue Boy* was not intended as a portrait, it is still a masterful description of a young teenager Gainsborough likely knew well. In his authoritative pose and tentative gaze, the figure displays the strange combination of swagger and uncertainty that characterises adolescence. The loss of this poignant image of youth on top of so many others lost in the war was seen in the light of a national tragedy. As if somehow to rectify the situation, the National Gallery purchased a well-known painting from the Panshanger collection, then thought to be a portrait of Lords John and Bernard Stuart by Van Dyck (now described as 'style of', NG3605), fearing it too would be sold to

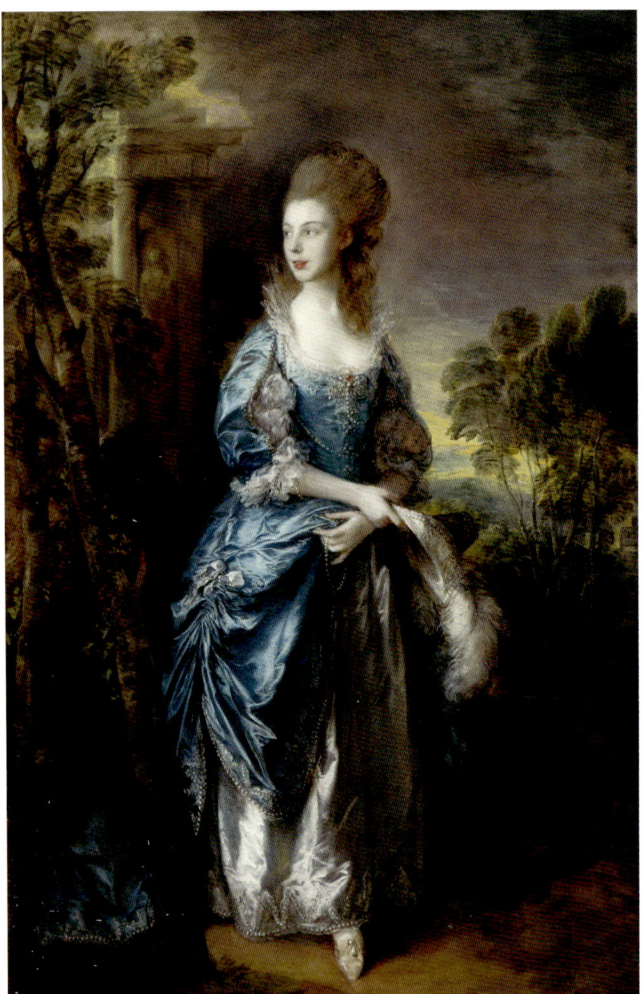

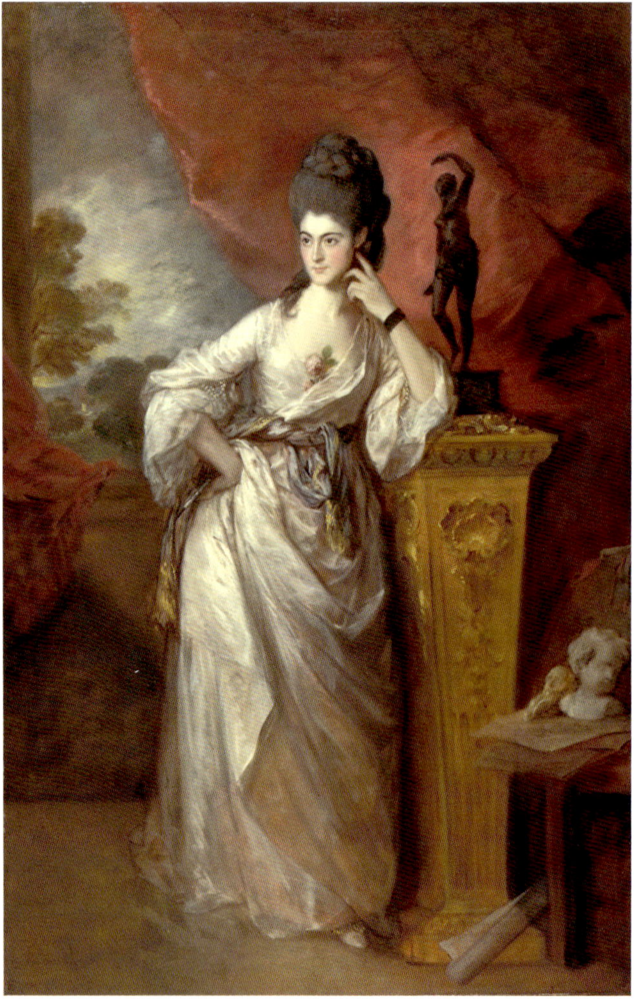

Fig. 26
Thomas Gainsborough (1727–1788)
The Hon. Frances Duncombe, about 1777
Oil on canvas, 234.3 x 155.3 cm
The Frick Collection, New York, Henry Clay Frick Bequest

Fig. 27
Thomas Gainsborough (1727–1788)
Penelope (Pitt), Viscountess Ligonier, 1770
Oil on canvas, 240 × 156.8 cm
The Huntington Library, Art Museum, and Botanical Gardens, San Marino, California

America.[11] The painting was quickly installed in the place *The Blue Boy* had recently occupied, and its acquisition was celebrated as a national triumph.[12] If *The Blue Boy* was the one that got away, at least a Van Dyck had been saved. Ironically, the National Gallery would acquire the actual portrait of the Stuart brothers in 1988 (cat. 4).

The reaction of the British public to *The Blue Boy*'s sale demonstrates how closely linked to British identity the painting had become. Cole Porter's song *Blue Boy Blues*, performed in the stage review *Mayfair and Montmartre* at London's New Oxford Theatre in the spring of 1922, contrasts the figure's character with that of the people among whom it would soon reside. In the song, the figure of *The Blue Boy* complains of his sale: 'A silver dollar took me and my collar/To show the slow cowboys/Just how boys/In England used to be dressed.'[13] Porter casts Gainsborough's reference to Van Dyck in the figure's blue satin breeches and embellished jacket as a marker of national character. The intended contrast is between his refinement and the rougher denizens of, as Porter put it, the 'Wild West'.

Among some commentators, the fact that *The Blue Boy* was going to the United States made its departure slightly more palatable. The author of 'A Farewell', for example, imagined giving comforting advice to the figure in the painting: 'We asked him … not to forget us, or cease to love us, but to love also the cousins overseas to whom he is bound, to speak to them of our common heritage, and to tell them that if he has to go, we would rather it were to them than to an alien race.'[14] It was perhaps in recognition of the 'special relationship' between the United Kingdom and the United States that, as *The Blue Boy* was being crated for shipping, Sir Charles Holmes took a pencil and inscribed on the painting's stretcher bar 'au revoir', in the hope of possible transatlantic visits 'home'.

American collectors were perhaps also thinking of this common heritage as they sought to fashion their identities through acquisitions. American financier J.P. Morgan had amassed an impressive collection of British old masters, including paintings by Reynolds, Gainsborough, Romney and Constable, which he had installed in his London residence. Other American collectors, such as Henry Clay Frick and Andrew Mellon, also included British paintings among their purchases. In 1911 Frick acquired Gainsborough's portrait of the Hon. Frances Duncombe (fig. 26), as well as two other British pictures by Romney and Raeburn. That same year Henry Huntington purchased three full-length portraits by Gainsborough, including that of Penelope, Viscountess Ligonier (fig. 27), and a double portrait by Romney in one transaction. Huntington was setting out on a clear path. Previously focused on building his library, Huntington began buying important examples of French decorative art in 1909. Now, however, he was in the market for top-quality pictures specifically from the British School. This new endeavour was undertaken largely under the influence of his uncle's widow, one of the greatest art collectors of her generation. It was Arabella Huntington who suggested the purchase of the Gainsborough and Romney portraits, and it was Arabella, not Henry, who negotiated the price.[15]

As Mrs Collis Huntington, Arabella had amassed an art collection that rivalled those of her contemporaries, including Morgan, Frick and Mellon. Like theirs, her collection combined paintings by the Continental old masters with eighteenth- and nineteenth-century British portraits, such as Reynolds's *Lady Charlotte Delaval Smith and her Children* (1787) and Thomas Lawrence's *Calmady Children* (1823), both now in the Metropolitan Museum of Art, New York. Arabella also owned a copy of *The Three Eldest Children of Charles I* by Van Dyck, which hung above the fireplace in the library of her New York home.[16] As discussed elsewhere in this book, Van Dyck's portraits of royal children inspired Gainsborough's depiction of courtly youth in *The Blue Boy*, a painting Arabella would also come to own during her second marriage to Henry Huntington.[17] Indeed, at the turn of the twentieth century, it was increasingly international art dealerships who paid vast sums for British portraits, being keen to foster such taste among their new clientele of American tycoons, who enjoyed what the art dealer Joseph Duveen referred to as these portraits' 'beauty', a term which encompassed the physical attractiveness of the elite subjects as well as the pictures' dashing painterliness and prestigious provenances.[18]

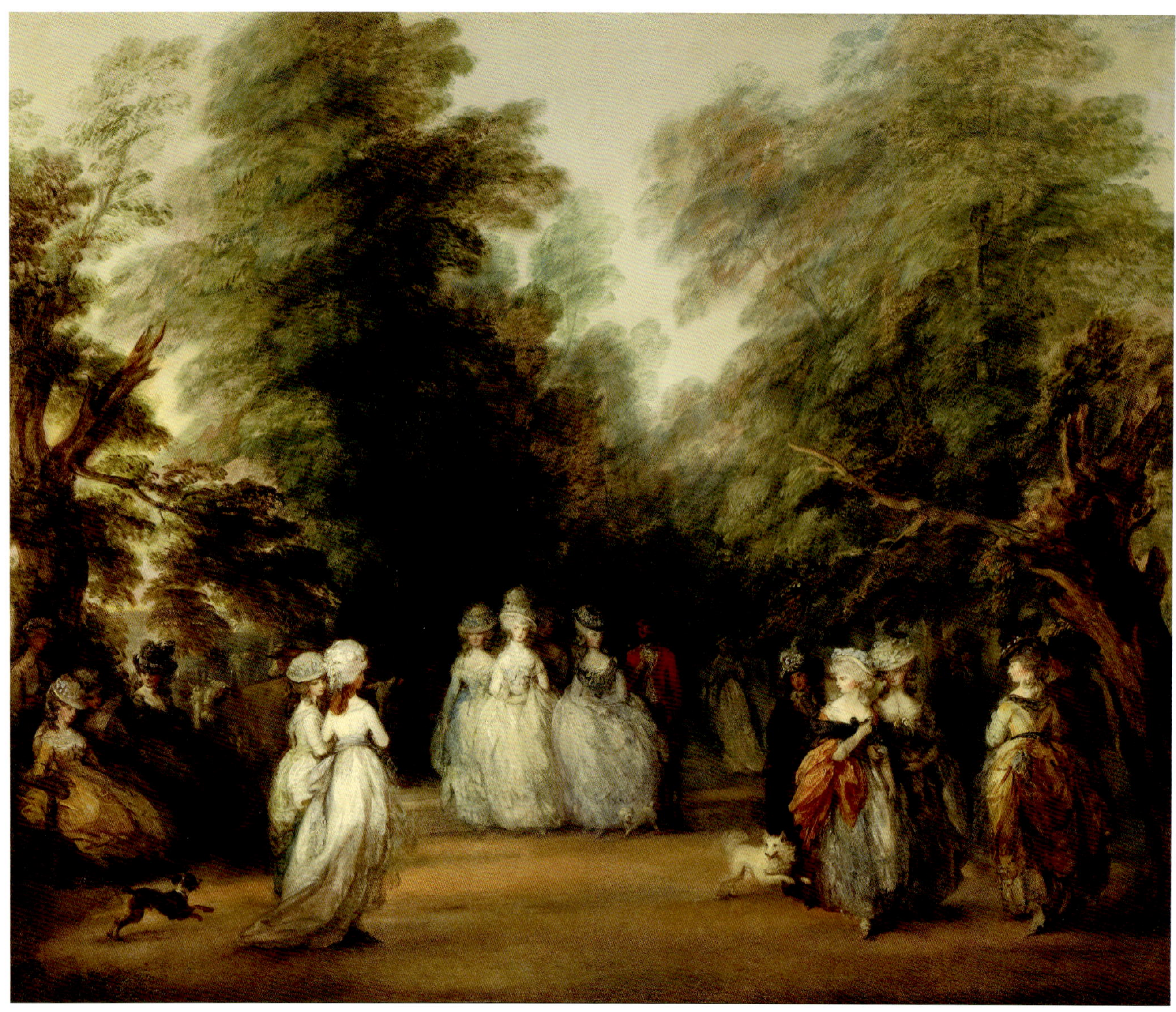

Fig. 28
Thomas Gainsborough (1727–1788)
The Mall in St James's Park, about 1783
Oil on canvas, 120.7 × 147 cm
The Frick Collection, New York, Henry Clay Frick Bequest

Fig. 29
Thomas Gainsborough (1727–1788)
Mrs Richard Brinsley Sheridan, 1785–7
Oil on canvas, 219.7 × 153.7 cm
National Gallery of Art, Washington, DC, Andrew W. Mellon Collection

In many ways, the Huntingtons' collection mirrors those of rival American collectors, such as Frick. Like him, they bought Asian ceramics, Italian Renaissance sculpture and eighteenth-century French furniture. However, while Frick purchased many British pictures, such as Gainsborough's *The Mall in St James's Park* (fig. 28), he was also buying a wide range of other old master paintings by artists like Titian, Vermeer, Bronzino and Boucher. With very few exceptions, the Huntingtons, by contrast, chose to focus on British paintings.

It was Arabella's son Archer who had advised the couple to limit their painting collection to one school.[19] At the time, a focus on British art was as practical as it was intellectual. In the early years of the twentieth century, two factors made collecting British art (indeed, the broad range of art found in British private collections) easier for Americans. While Morgan had likely kept his collection in London to avoid steep import duties, later collectors, such as the Huntingtons,

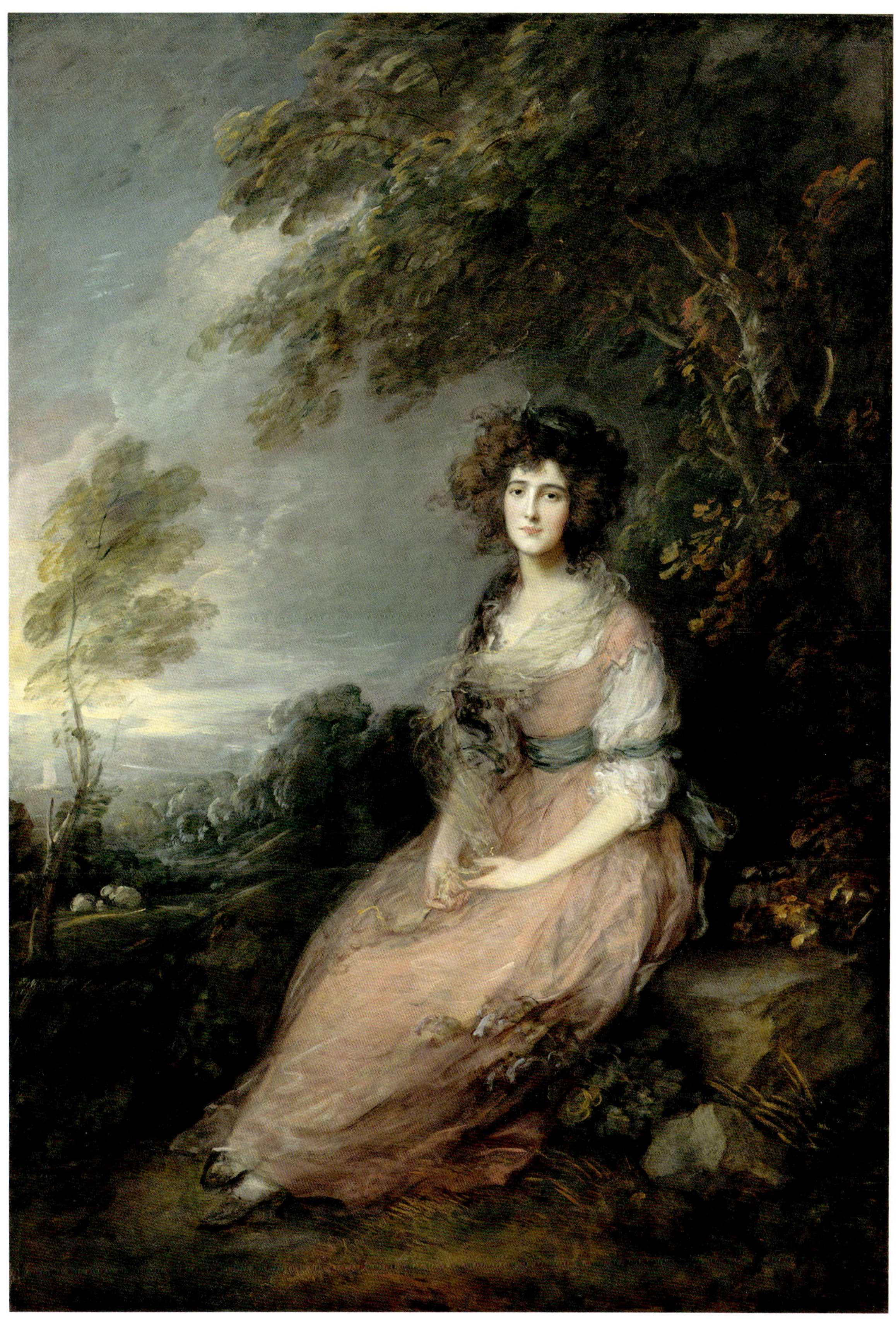

benefited from a 1909 US law that repealed tariffs on works of art over one hundred years old imported into the United States.[20] Additionally, a significant increase in inheritance, land and income taxes enacted in the United Kingdom in 1910 forced many members of the British gentry and aristocracy to sell portions of their moveable property in order to pay. Often, it was art that was sacrificed. On both sides of the Atlantic, tax laws contributed to a massive cultural exchange, putting many treasures from British collections on the market, and allowing wealthy Americans to bring them home.

If works from British collections established many of the greatest art collections in America, the collections themselves also served as models for their American counterparts. Frick and Huntington based their future museums on aristocratic private-turned-public collections such as The Wallace Collection. Andrew Mellon, on the other hand, had ideas on a grander scale. His vision for a national gallery of art for the United States was rooted in the collection in Trafalgar Square. Mellon, who had been making regular extended visits to the United Kingdom for 50 years, modelled his own collection of art on what he saw at the National Gallery. According to his aide, David Finley, who would later become the American museum's first director, 'Everything there appealed to him: the size, the installation, the high level of quality.'[21] Like Britain's National Gallery, Mellon's collection featured a broad range of old master works, including paintings by many British artists. Among his works gifted to the National Gallery of Art, which he established in Washington, DC, were 21 British pictures by artists such as Reynolds, Romney, Lawrence, Constable and Turner, as well as five paintings by Gainsborough, including his portrait of Mrs Richard Brinsley Sheridan (fig. 29). Also in the gift were five portraits by Van Dyck, among them *Susanna Fourment and her Daughter* (1621, National Gallery of Art, Washington, DC).

Although the ease with which works of art from British collections could now be acquired had greatly increased the rate at which American collectors were buying them, the cultural status of the sellers themselves was an added attraction. The expansion of the economy after the end of the American Civil War (1861–5) created a new class of millionaires whose fortunes were based in industry and the financial institutions that supported it. What these rising tycoons lacked was the perceived authority and social position conferred upon their European counterparts through lineage. Many of them came from modest backgrounds. Arabella Huntington, for example, was the daughter of a machinist. She became the mistress of railroad magnate Collis Huntington while still in her teens, marrying him on the death of his first wife. Henry worked his way up in his uncle's company, eventually holding several leadership positions, before investing on his own in Southern California real estate and public transportation systems. In the late nineteenth century, wealthy Americans such as the Huntingtons began building lavish residences and collecting works of art as a means of acquiring cultural status. In buying artwork from British collections, particularly works of the British School, American collectors were also drawing upon the 'cousinly' connection shared by the United States and the United Kingdom. In the case of Andrew Mellon's son, whose later collecting activities established the Yale Center for British Art in New Haven, Connecticut, the connection was literal: Paul Mellon's mother was British.[22] Although the existence of a purely Anglo-American identity for the United States was little more than a myth, British portraits, more than anything else, implied a historic lineage for their owners. When Henry and Arabella Huntington purchased *The Blue Boy* (along with Reynolds's *Sarah Siddons as the Tragic Muse* and Gainsborough's *Cottage Door*) from the Duke of Westminster, they were buying the intellectual and cultural status endowed through the ownership of fine art as well as the paintings' illustrious provenance.

American audiences were personally introduced to *The Blue Boy* at Duveen's New York showroom, where it was placed on public exhibition for three weeks upon its arrival in the United States. As it had in London, the painting's exhibition in New York elicited an emotional response from visitors: 'there was something of the reverence of one of the quiet chapels of a medieval cathedral, where among the silent worshippers there lurks the presence of a Master'.[23] The painting's progress across the continent by train to the Huntington 'ranch' was marked by the press, which noted the security arrangements that accompanied it.[24] Although Henry and Arabella Huntington had purchased *The Blue Boy* with the intention of installing it in their private residence, they had already signed in 1919 the trust indenture that would make the collection a public one after their deaths. When the Huntington collection opened in 1928 as part of the Henry E. Huntington Library and Art Gallery (now the Huntington Library, Art Museum, and Botanical Gardens), it was the first public museum of old master art in Southern California. It soon became one of the region's most popular attractions, no doubt due in part to the fame of *The Blue Boy*, which had been joined by another icon of British portraiture, Lawrence's *Sarah Goodin Barrett Moulton* (1794), otherwise known as '*Pinkie*', in 1927 (fig. 39).

The Blue Boy was now part of the artistic landscape of Southern California, and well on its way to becoming an icon of American popular culture. It was aided in this by the Huntington's proximity to Hollywood. Images of *The Blue Boy* have appeared in film productions since the medium's earliest days. It has shared the screen with characters as diverse as Laurel and Hardy, and Batman. James Bond, played by Pierce Brosnan, damaged the canvas during a fencing match in *Die Another Day* (2002). And actor Jamie Foxx dressed in a very familiar blue suit as the title character of Quentin Tarantino's *Django Unchained* (2012).[25] In addition to movies, television brought *The Blue Boy* to American audiences, right in the comfort of their living rooms. It appeared every week on the wall of the Cleavers' home in the hit 1950s sitcom *Leave it to Beaver*, where it signalled the family's status as typical members of America's middle class. As in Britain, cheap reproductions proliferated, along with a dizzying array of crafts and collectible items, from needlepoint kits to shot glasses, now ensuring a place for the painting in the American collective consciousness.[26] Over

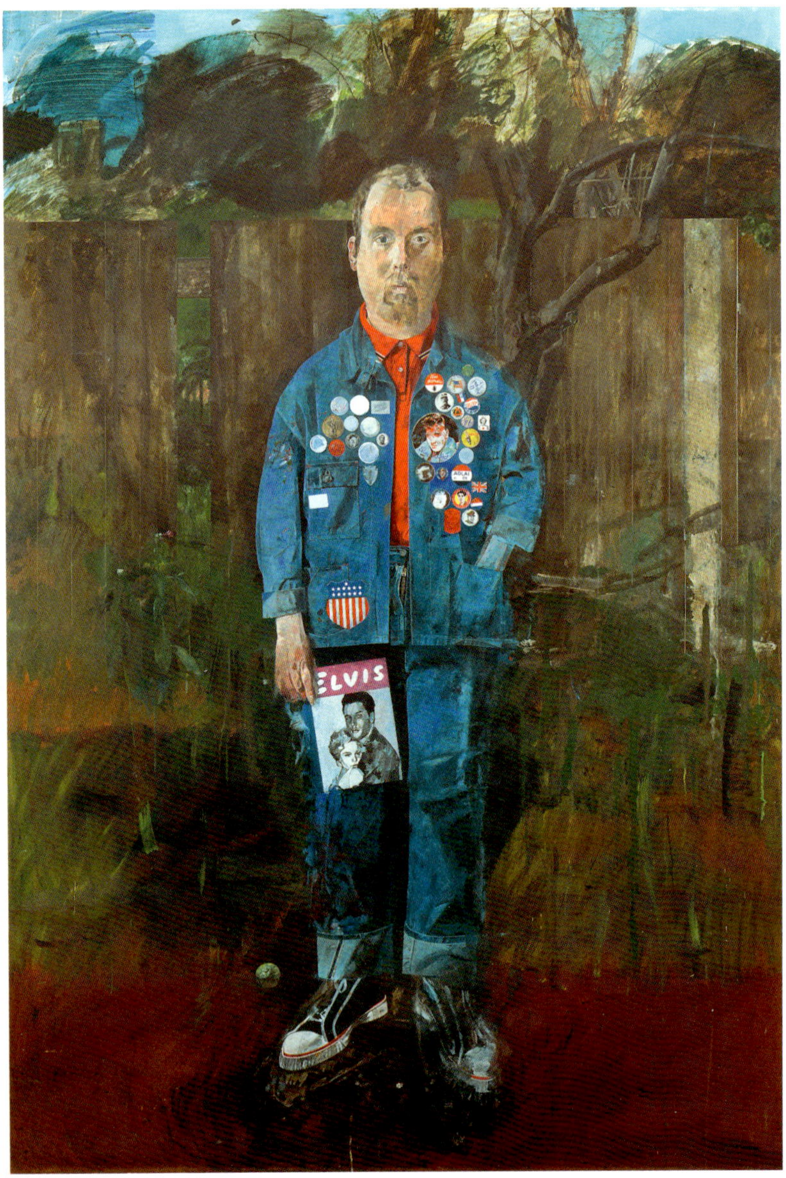

Fig. 30
Peter Blake (born 1932)
Self-portrait with Badges, 1961
Oil on board, 174.3 × 121.9 cm
Tate, London, presented by the Moores Family Charitable Foundation to celebrate the John Moores Liverpool Exhibition 1979

the course of the twentieth century, *The Blue Boy* participated in the building of a shared American cultural identity through mass consumerism.

Deeply rooted in American popular culture, *The Blue Boy*, and by extension British art, continued to serve as a touchstone for creativity. A young Robert Rauschenberg, on furlough from the US Navy during the Second World War, visited the Huntington Art Gallery, where the experience of viewing '*Pinkie*', *Sarah Siddons* and *The Blue Boy* changed the course of his life: 'My moment of realization that there was such a thing as being an artist happened right there.'[27] Kehinde Wiley had a similar experience four decades later, when the 'sheer spectacle, and of course beauty' he saw in these same paintings inspired his career as a visual artist.[28] British art also continued to reckon with Gainsborough's iconic image. In the 1960s Peter Blake transformed *The Blue Boy* from pop icon into icon of pop art. The artist presented a very different image of British identity in his *Self-portrait with Badges* (1961). His scruffy, middle-aged figure turns Gainsborough's image of gilded youth on its head; at the same time, his brushwork captures the rough texture of denim as deftly as Gainsborough mimicked the look of blue satin (fig. 30). Alex Israel, on the other hand, asserted a strongly Southern Californian image for *The Blue Boy* in his own self portrait, where the shimmering blue of a Los Angeles Dodgers baseball jacket stands in for the figure's Van Dyck suit (fig. 31).

By the end of the twentieth century, *The Blue Boy* seemed almost as American as it was British. Now, the painting has returned to the National Gallery, where it once again takes its place as an icon of British art. In many ways, the United Kingdom is a different nation from the one it left, no longer the centre of a global empire, but with a population that reflects that past more than it did in 1922, a nation now seeking to redefine its place in a post-Brexit world. What will *The Blue Boy* mean for this Britain? Audiences a century ago admired Gainsborough's artistry, but they *responded* to the boy they saw in the painting. And although the canvas has recently undergone conservation treatment to reveal the dazzling brushwork long hidden beneath layers of dirt, overpaint and cloudy varnish, perhaps the

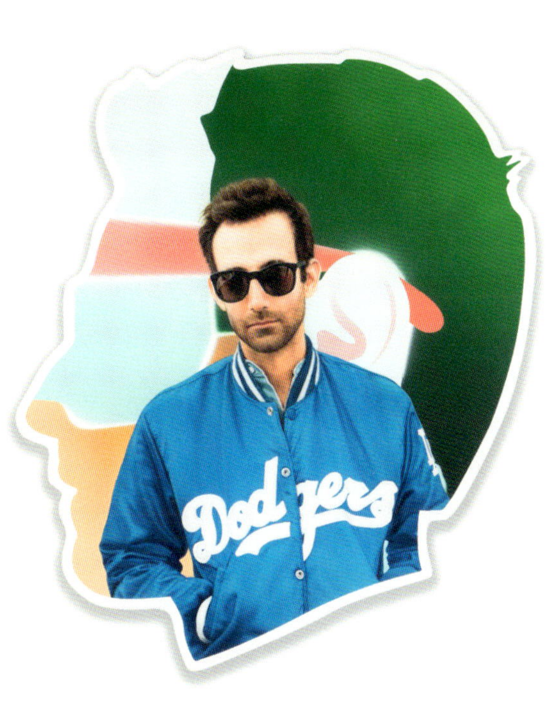

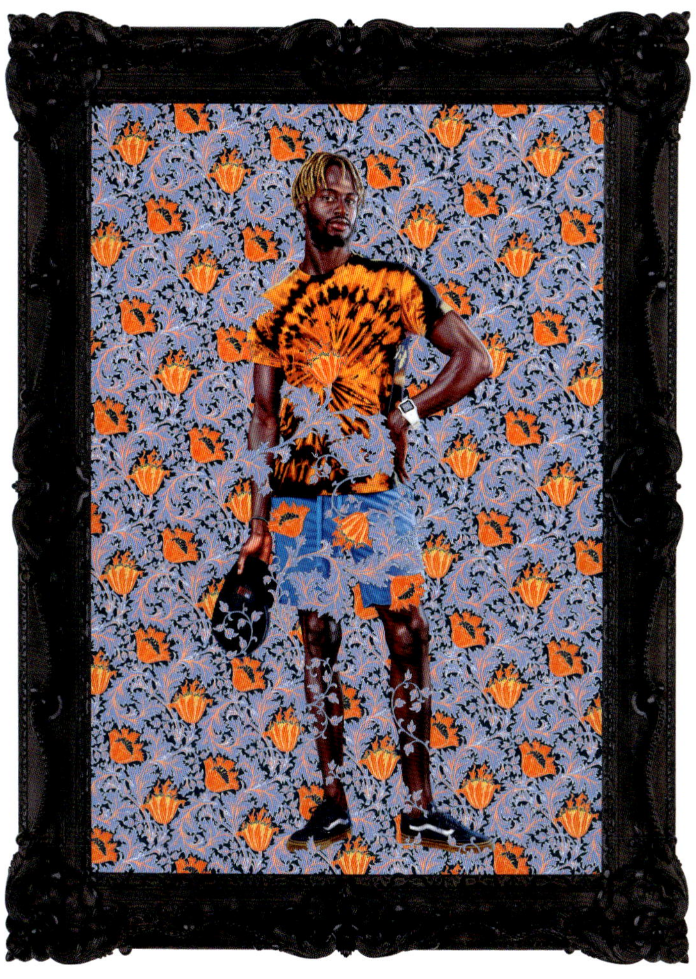

Fig. 31
Alex Israel (born 1982)
Self-portrait (Dodgers), 2014–15
Acrylic and bondo on fibreglass,
243.8 x 213.4 × 10.1 cm
Collection of the artist

Fig. 32
Kehinde Wiley (born 1977)
A Portrait of a Young Gentleman, 2021
Oil on linen with wooden frame,
218.7 x 165.1 x 12.7 cm
Collection of The Huntington Library, Art Museum, and Botanical Gardens; and Commissioned through Roberts Projects, Los Angeles; Gift of Anne F. Rothenberg, Terry Perucca and Annette Serrurier, the Philip and Muriel Berman Foundation, Laura and Carlton Seaver, Kent Belden and Dr Louis Re, and Faye and Robert Davidson

answer still lies in the figure itself. In October 2021 a new painting by Kehinde Wiley, based on Gainsborough's composition, debuted at the Huntington, commissioned by the institution to mark the centenary of *The Blue Boy*'s acquisition. The model for this new 'Blue Boy' was to have been chosen from the streets of Los Angeles, where the artist grew up and where the painting now resides. However, Wiley began the work during the pandemic of 2020, which he spent at his residence in Dakar, Senegal. The figure in Wiley's version of *The Blue Boy* is Senegalese. His model is also several years older, fully embodying the swagger not quite achieved by Gainsborough's teen. Wiley's *A Portrait of a Young Gentleman* (fig. 32) proclaims a new identity for *The Blue Boy* that is Black, self-assured and globally oriented; at the same time it reiterates the power of the original. That power comes from the grand manner format, which has been adapted to endow sitters from kings to children with visual authority and attention-grabbing presence. It also comes from Gainsborough's ability to characterise humanity, which viewers have recognised, and identified with, in *The Blue Boy* across different times and cultures. His image of an anonymous teenager on the cusp of adulthood, full of confidence yet touched with uncertainty, is a testament of youth and of the potential it represents.

Catalogue Entries

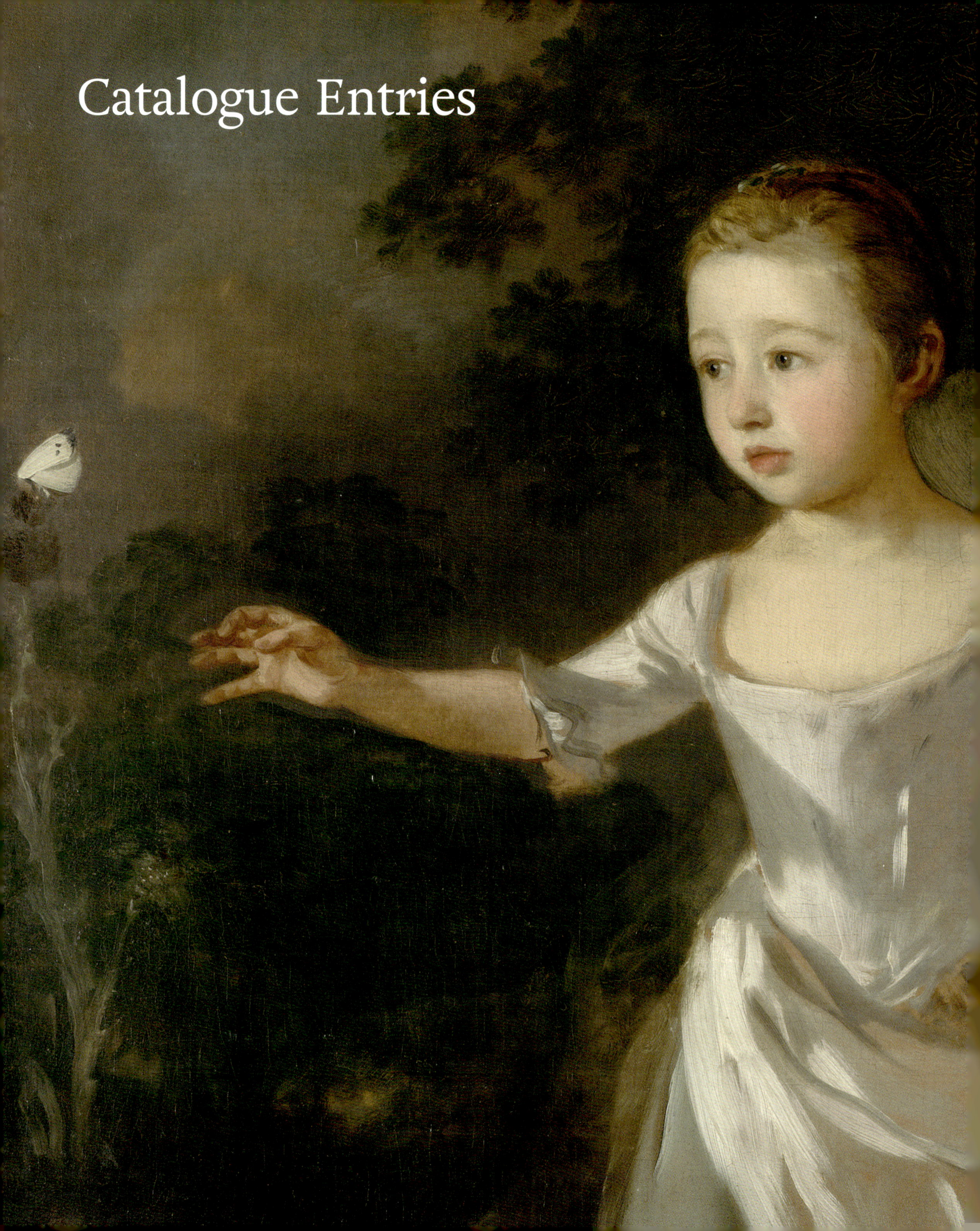

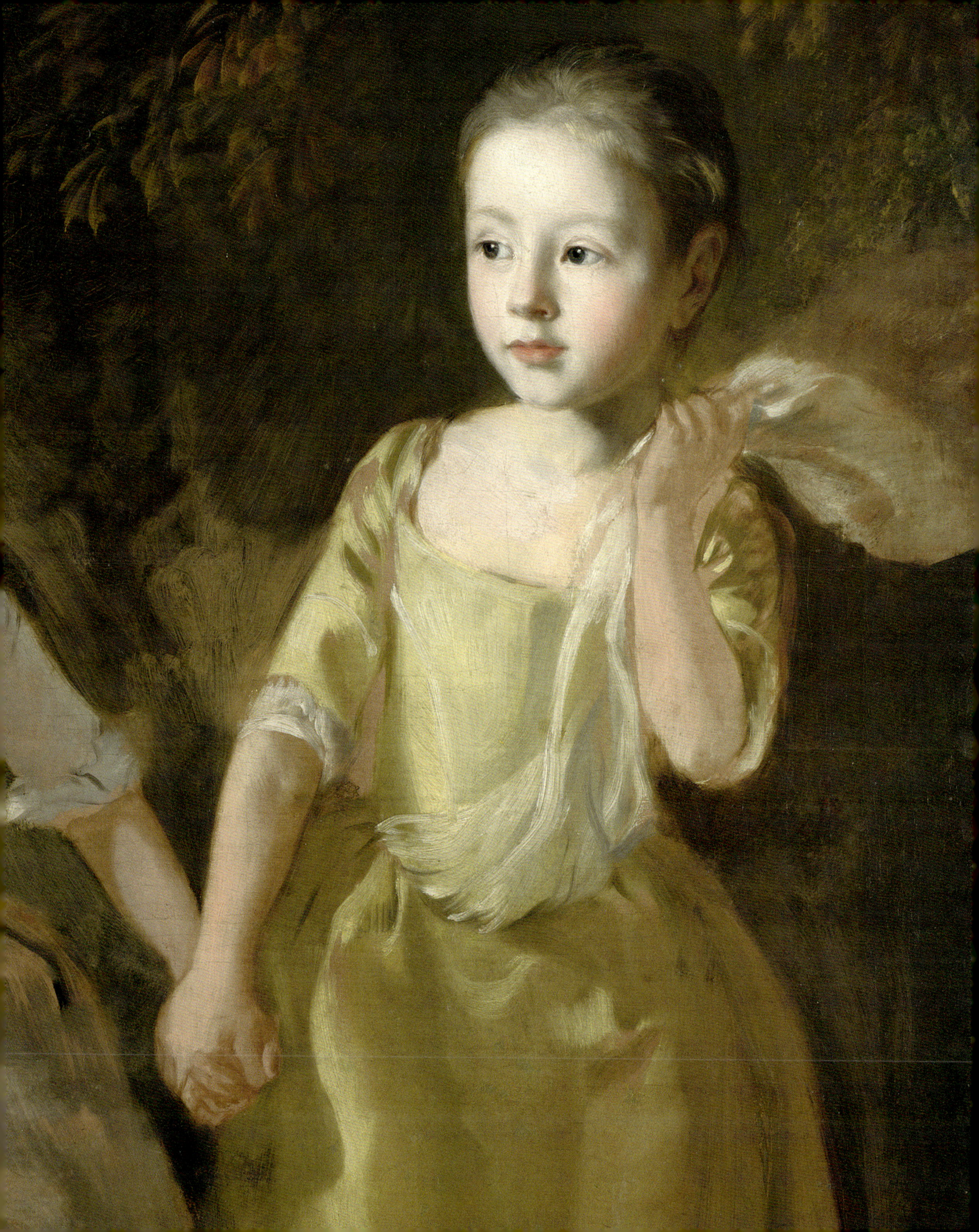

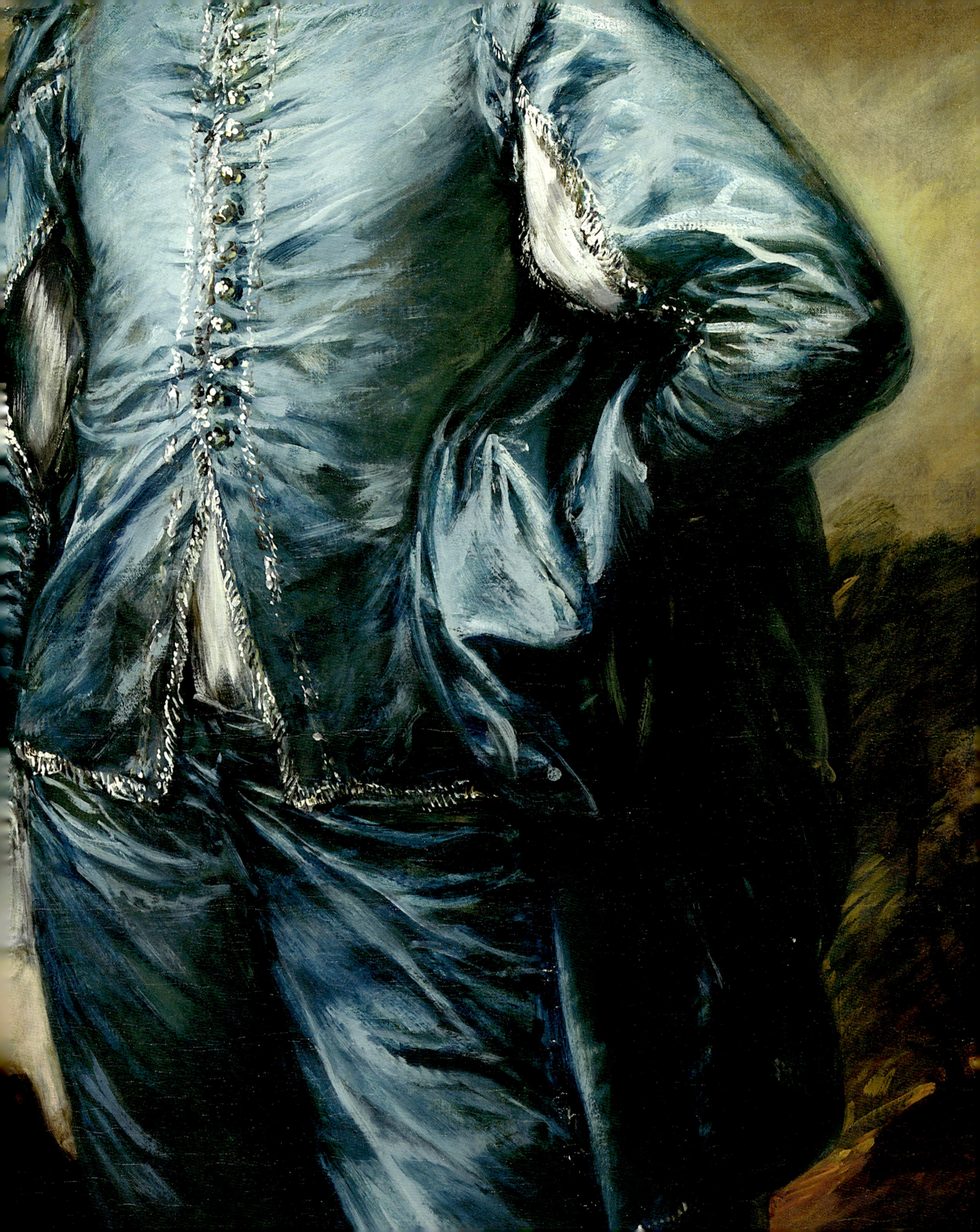

1

Thomas Gainsborough (1727–1788)

The Blue Boy, about 1770

Oil on canvas, 179.4 × 123.8 cm
The Huntington Library, Art Museum,
and Botanical Gardens, San Marino, California (21.1)

The Blue Boy is the product of Thomas Gainsborough's allegiance to Anthony van Dyck, the seventeenth-century Flemish painter on whose practice he modelled his own. It depicts a boy dressed in a blue satin 'Van Dyck' suit, a studio prop owned by the artist that appears in several portraits, including those depicting his nephews, Gainsborough Dupont and Edward Richard Gardner.[1] The figure faces the viewer, a black feathered hat in his right hand, his left arm akimbo. His pale face and shimmering clothing stand out against a dark landscape. His head and torso rise above a low horizon, set off by a cloud-filled sky. The figure's pose is based on that of George Villiers in Van Dyck's double portrait *George Villiers, 2nd Duke of Buckingham (1628–1687) and Lord Francis Villiers (1629–1648)* (cat. 5), lending the composition the gravity of a royal commission. *The Blue Boy*, however, was not a commissioned work. Gainsborough reused a canvas, cut down from an abandoned full-length portrait, and employed an anonymous model instead of a recognisable sitter.[2] Exhibited in 1770 as *A Portrait of a Young Gentleman*, the painting is a showpiece made to announce its creator as the heir to Van Dyck's legacy.

To achieve this goal, *The Blue Boy* had to stand apart from Gainsborough's contemporaries. Sir Joshua Reynolds had been lending his portraits a 'historick air' with Van Dyck's poses or employing associated dress prior to 1770,[3] including portraits of young boys, such as *Jacob Bouverie, 2nd Earl of Radnor* (1757, private collection) and *George Capel, Viscount Malden and his Sister, Lady Elizabeth Capel* (1768, Metropolitan Museum of Art, New York). George Romney also painted youthful cavaliers, such as John Sayer, who sports his school's famed archery dress (1770, Harrow School).[4] X-rays show that Gainsborough originally included a dog in *The Blue Boy*.[5] Placed at the model's feet, the fluffy white spaniel was painted over by the artist prior to the painting's exhibition.[6] The change created a single, monumental figure, which now commanded the canvas with a steady, direct gaze calculated to draw attention.[7] Reynolds would later employ a similar strategy in his portrait of Prince William Frederick (1780, Trinity College, Cambridge), in which the young prince, dressed in lilac Van Dyck satin, adopts the pose seen in the Flemish painter's celebrated *Charles I at the Hunt* (about 1635, Musée du Louvre, Paris).

Reynolds criticised the use of Van Dyck costume in contemporary portraiture, claiming such superficial associations ignored the artist's 'real excellence'.[8] That 'excellence' referred to Van Dyck's painterly skill, manifested in his celebrated 'brilliant' effect and almost legendary speed of execution.[9] Gainsborough strove to replicate this brilliancy in his own work by mastering Van Dyck's virtuosic technique and transparent application. For example, the unfinished portrait of his nephew, Gainsborough Dupont (fig. 33), employs a combination of short, hatching strokes seen in the face, energetic touches in the hair, and broad swathes of colour, as in the collar, over multiple thin glazes that allow light to penetrate and reflect off the bright ground layer, lending the figure striking luminosity. These same elements are present in *The Blue Boy*, visible especially in the costume, where transparent layers of varying blue pigments build upon each other to create a complex structure of bold slashes and delicate strokes that refract light, making the figure appear to glow from within. Unlike Reynolds, whose primary links to Van Dyck were through costume or pose, Gainsborough could emulate Van Dyck's touch, a clear signifier of his status as artistic successor. Equally some of Gainsborough's portraits, including *Ignatius Sancho* (1768, National Gallery of Canada, Ottawa), were described by commentators as being produced at virtuosic speed, mirroring similarly admiring descriptions of Van Dyck.[10] Made to establish its painter's place among British artists, *The Blue Boy* is thus a portrait of its own creator, an image of allegiance, ambition and artistry. MM

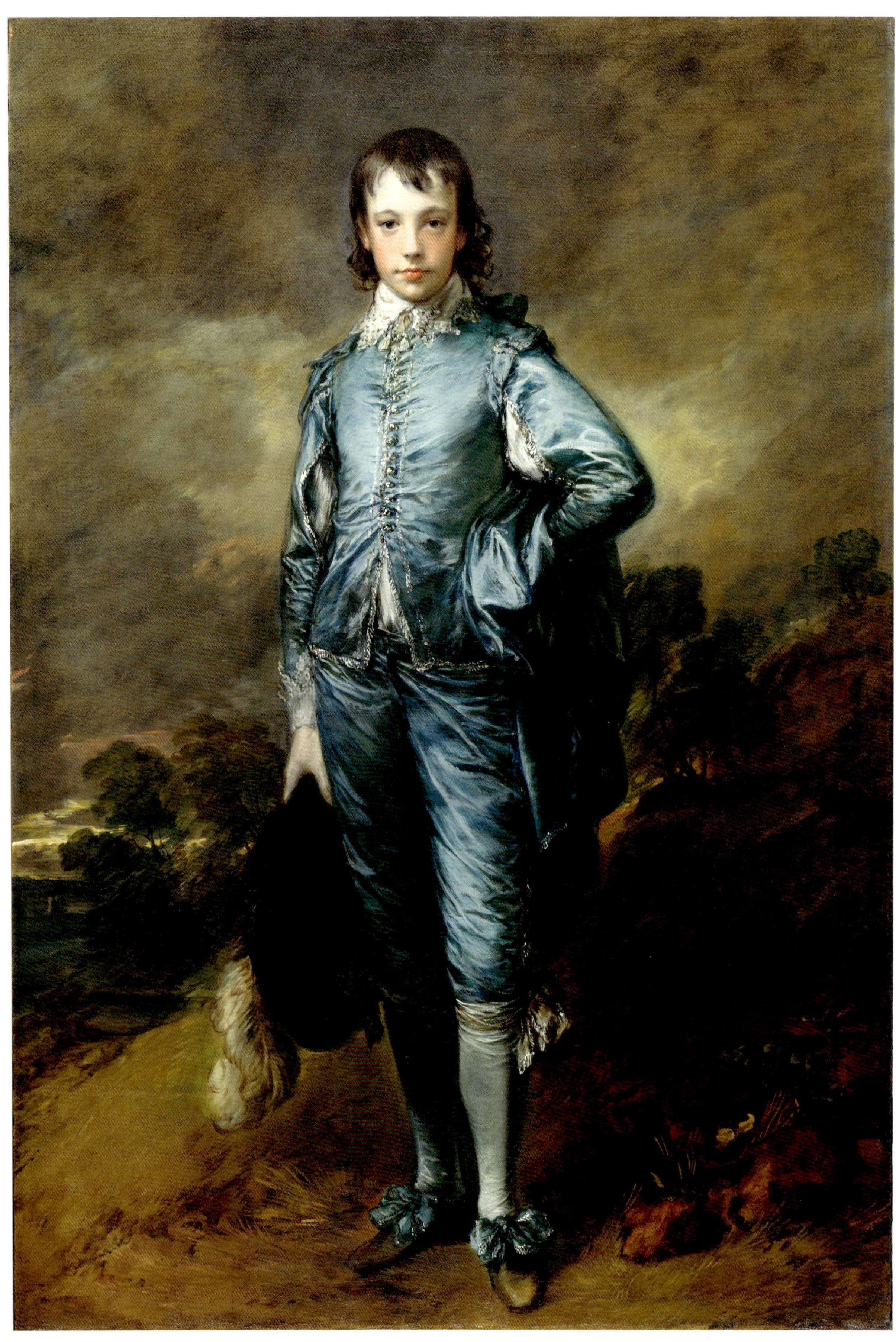

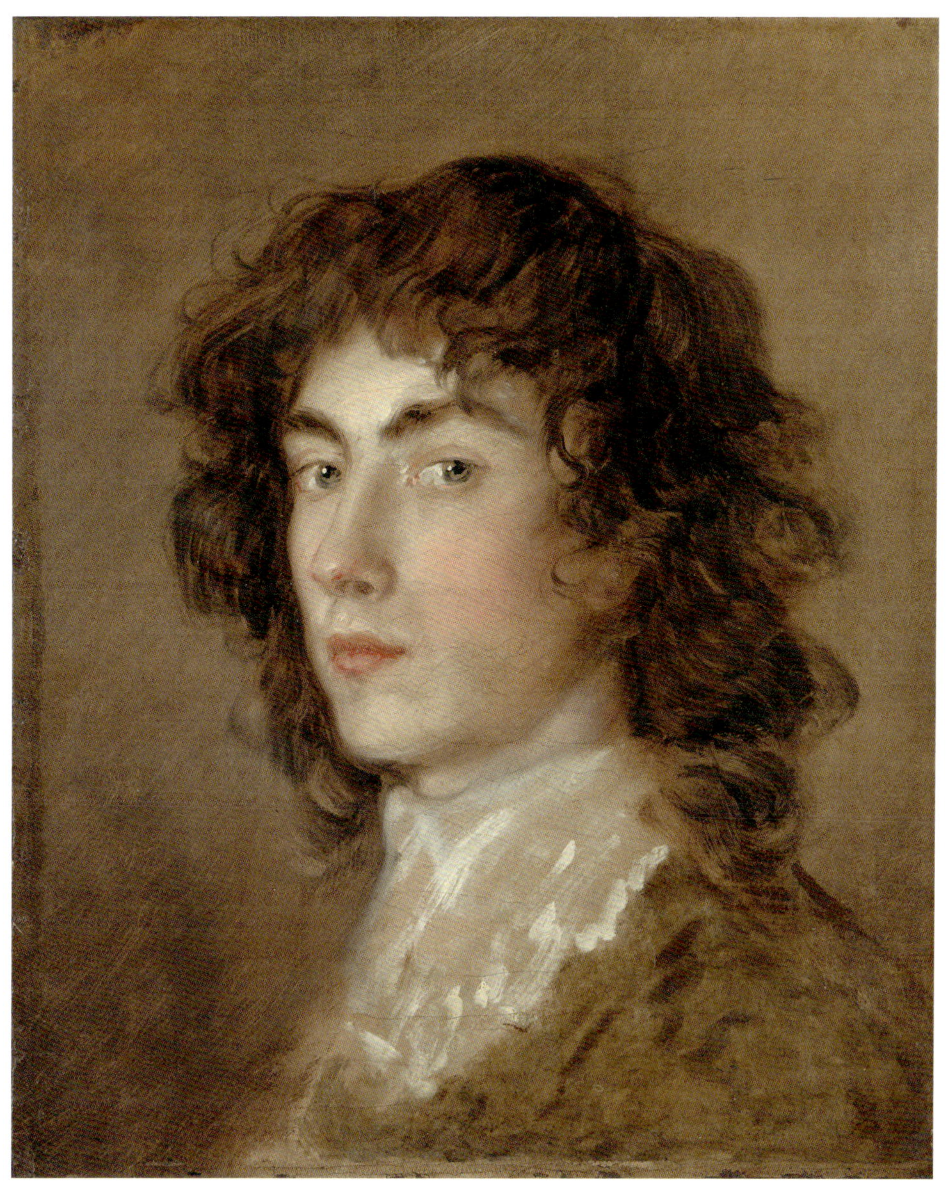

Fig. 33
Thomas Gainsborough (1727–1788)
Gainsborough Dupont, about 1770–5
Oil on canvas, 45.5 × 37.5 cm
Tate, London. Bequeathed by Lady d'Abernon 1954

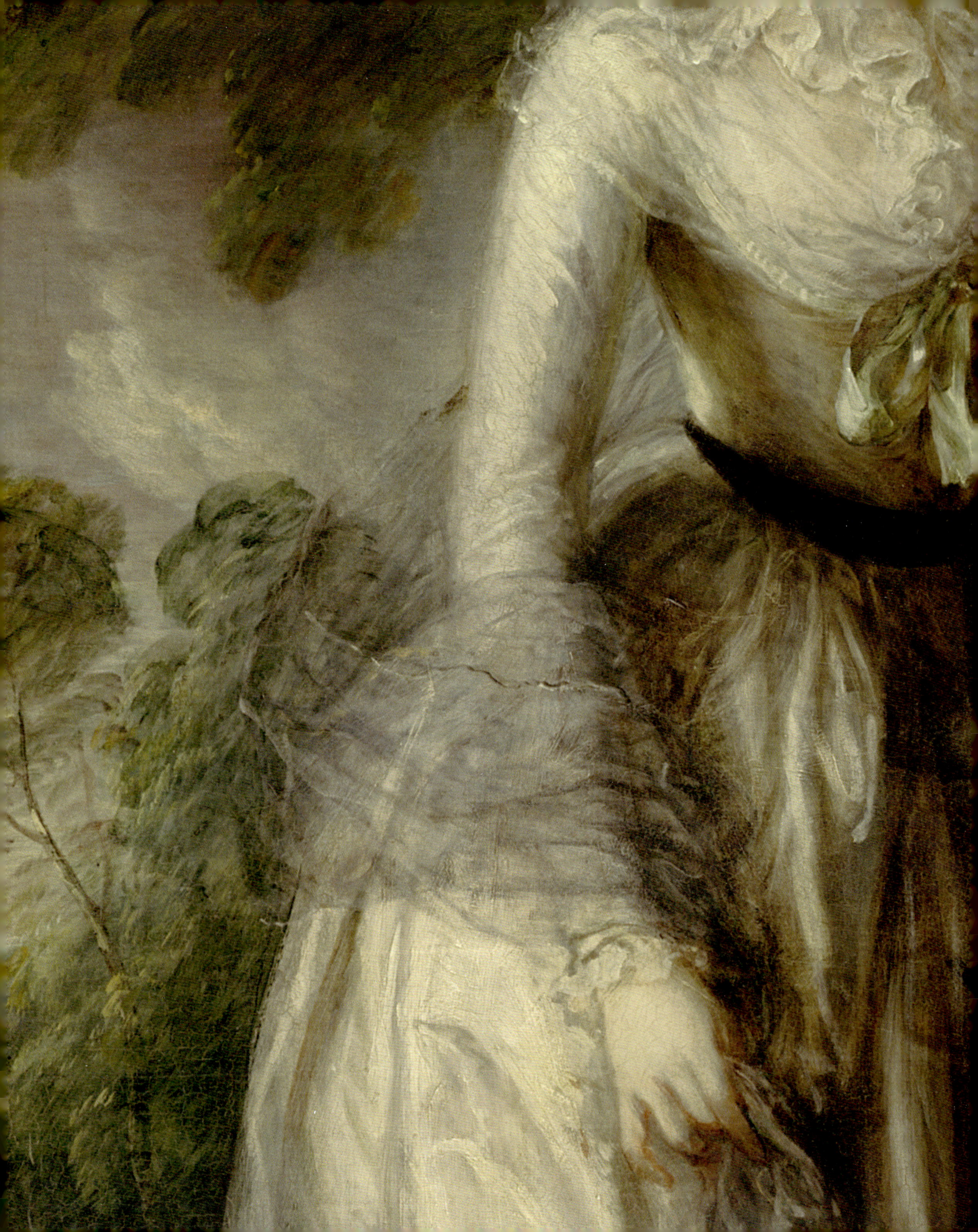

2

Thomas Gainsborough (1727–1788)

Mr and Mrs William Hallett ('The Morning Walk'), 1785

Oil on canvas, 236.2 × 179.1 cm
The National Gallery, London (NG6209)

Gainsborough painted the portrait of William Hallett and Elizabeth Stephen before their marriage in 1785. The couple are shown in fashionable dress taking a stroll in a romanticised setting, accompanied by a Pomeranian sheepdog. The feathery brushwork, typical of the artist's late style, adds a sense of movement through the slanting strokes in the sky and foliage. The result is a picture that is remarkable for its refined poetic quality, both as a portrait of young love and of individual likenesses.

It has been suggested that this and other late portraits, including *Lady Sheffield* (1785, Waddesdon Manor, Buckinghamshire) and *Mrs Richard Brinsley Sheridan* (fig. 29), should be viewed as 'fancy pictures' rather than straightforward portraits. This may in part stem from its title, *The Morning Walk*, a reference to James Thomson's influential poem *The Seasons* (1730), but probably not associated with this painting until around 1884, when it was acquired by a member of the Rothschild family (see pp. 30–1).[1] In the same year, however, Gainsborough painted the ambitious 'fancy picture' *The Cottage Girl* (1785, National Gallery of Ireland, Dublin) and a few years later *Haymaker and Sleeping Girl* (about 1788, Museum of Fine Arts, Boston), both painted on a scale normally reserved for grand full-length portraits.[2]

Only months before his death, Gainsborough wrote, 'I feel such a fondness for my first imitations of the little Dutch Landskips.'[3] This underscores that the artist periodically looked back to earlier influences, often to reinvigorate his art, while extending his range of old master references to Rembrandt, Murillo and Claude. Gainsborough's *The Rt Hon. Charles Wolfran Cornwell* (1785–6, National Gallery of Victoria, Melbourne) refers back to William Hogarth's *Captain Thomas Coram* and Allan Ramsay's *Dr Richard Mead* from the 1740s (see p. 11).[4] And the idyllic urban scene, *The Mall in St James's Park* (fig. 28), recalls Antoine Watteau. The motif of strolling figures in poetical landscapes, for which Watteau was renowned, can also be seen in *The Morning Walk* and other paintings of this period.[5]

The overall effect and scale of *The Morning Walk* contrasts dramatically with *Mr and Mrs Andrews* (fig. 34), which has often been described as a triple portrait of a husband, wife and estate. The scene itself melds different genres – sporting art, conversation piece and landscape – with Gainsborough's skilful rendering of weather conditions and naturalistic scenery, influenced by seventeenth-century Dutch painting (see pp. 10–11). Taken together, these two portraits, spanning some 35 years, both demonstrate Gainsborough's enduring attachment to rural scenes, while revealing just how far his painting had developed and transformed.

One prominent influence which is absent from *Mr and Mrs Andrews*, but evident in *The Morning Walk*, is that of Van Dyck: for example, in the delicate harmony of the couple's poses and gestures, and in the predominance of black with a hint of white in one costume, which is then reversed in the other. Equally, Gainsborough increasingly applied thin paint layers in a 'hatching' manner, a technique then firmly associated with Van Dyck and Rubens. Interestingly, there seems to be only one published review during Gainsborough's lifetime that links him and Van Dyck by name. This changed after his death, with the obituarist in the *Morning Chronicle* claiming that Gainsborough was the only contemporary artist in England to paint in the 'thin, brilliant style of pencilling of Vandyke [sic]'.[6] Such references were, of course, flattering to Gainsborough, but they also formed part of an ongoing debate around technique and durability, with Gainsborough's supporters highlighting his superiority in this regard over the experimentations of Reynolds – largely in pursuit of old master effects – with results that were short-lived and colours 'flying off' (fading).[7] CR

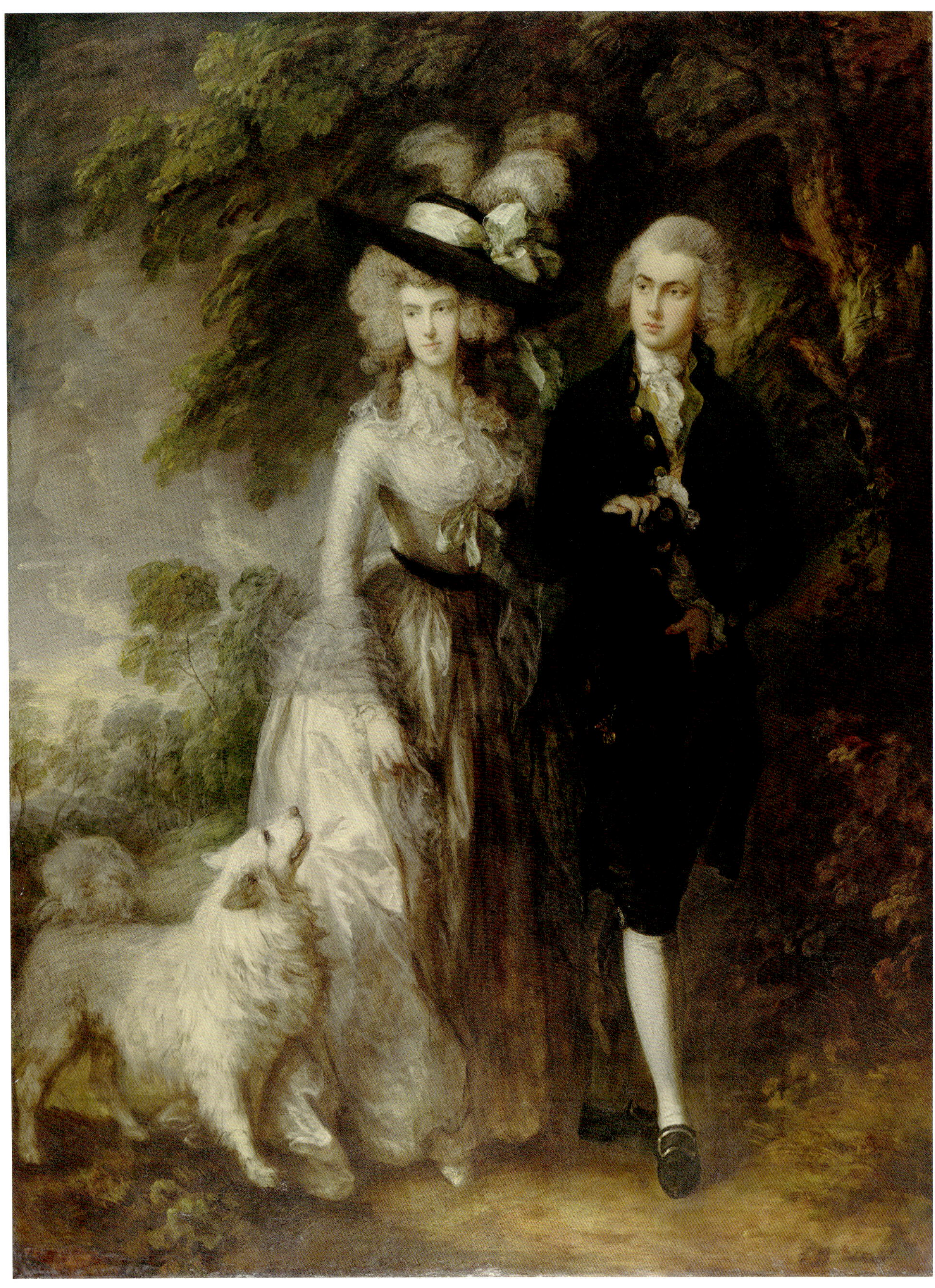

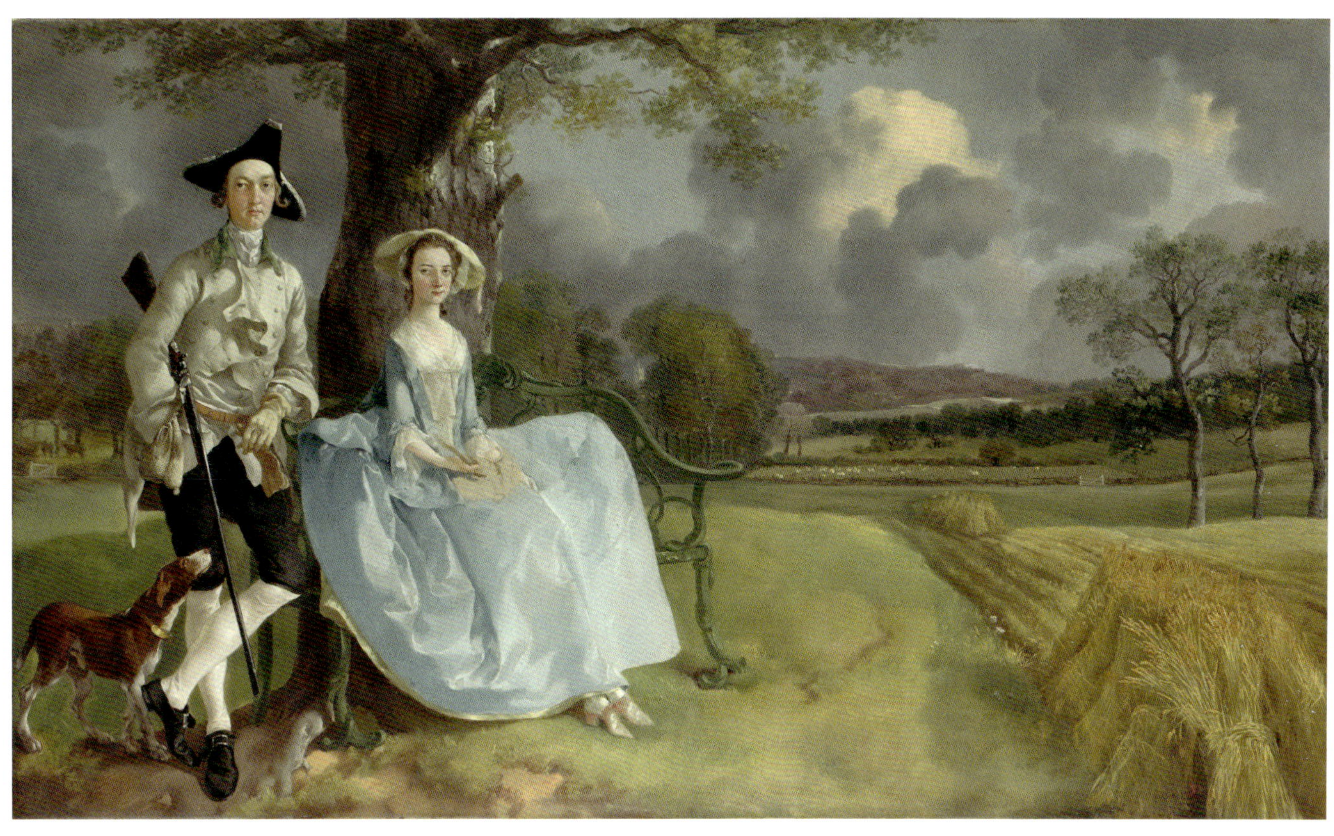

Fig. 34
Thomas Gainsborough (1727–1788)
Mr and Mrs Andrews, about 1750
Oil on canvas, 69.8 × 119.4 cm
The National Gallery, London

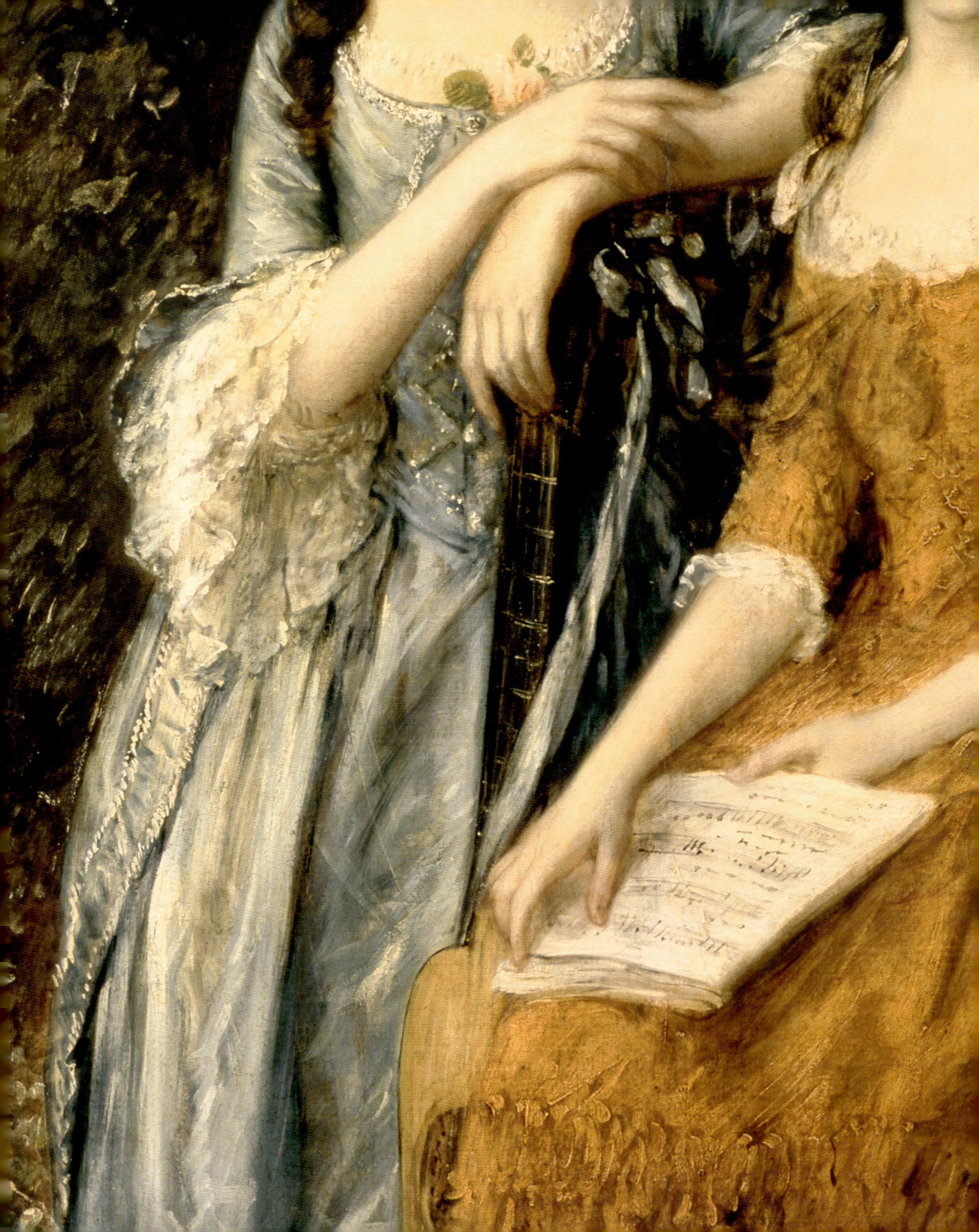

3

Thomas Gainsborough (1727–1788)

Elizabeth and Mary Linley, about 1772, retouched 1785

Oil on canvas, 199 × 153.5 cm
Dulwich Picture Gallery, London (DPG320)

Gainsborough undertook this double portrait when he was living in Bath, probably as a gift to the sitters' father, his close friend Thomas Linley, a music professor and concert director. Gainsborough had known these women since they were girls. Elizabeth was already a celebrated professional singer and actress, and in early 1771, when this portrait was begun, her younger sister Mary joined her on the stage. The painting was nearly complete in 1772 when Elizabeth eloped to France with the playwright Richard Brinsley Sheridan. Later that year it was exhibited at the Royal Academy, where a critic for the *London Chronicle* remarked that the 'draperies are well cast and the lights sweetly distributed'.[1]

The sisters are discovered in a leafy garden, holding a beribboned guitar and a stack of sheet music. The outdoor setting and musical props recall Watteau's *fêtes galantes* – paintings that present elegant lovers in pastoral landscapes – as well as the theatrical tradition of *commedia dell'arte* and the 'Arcadian' masques associated with the Stuart court in England.[2] These items also signal the sisters' vocation as singers: by this date, guitars were often used to accompany the voice. However, as opera and oratorio singers, the Linley sisters would not have sung to guitar accompaniment, and neither sitter is known to have played the instrument. It is therefore likely that the guitar belonged to Gainsborough, an enthusiastic amateur musician, who played several instruments.[3]

Like *Mrs Siddons* (cat. 6), the sisters' portrait eschews theatrical costume for contemporary dress. Such was the Linleys' preoccupation with fashion that in 1785, the family asked Gainsborough to retouch the sisters' hairstyles and dress to bring their clothes up to date: the girls were given a shawl and a fringed scarf, tresses were added over their shoulders and Elizabeth's ears were covered.[4] Gainsborough's lively brushwork captures the delicate cream sheen on Elizabeth's blue dress with a fluidity that attests to his ambitions to paint in the manner of Van Dyck, as well as to borrow his costumes and attitudes. Sir Joshua Reynolds recalled how Gainsborough paid close attention to Van Dyck's painterly technique in his colouring and use of light and shade.[5] The contrasting poses and colours, between Mary's russet dress and Elizabeth's pale blue, emulate Van Dyck's *Stuart Brothers* (cat. 4), which Gainsborough knew intimately.

Soon after he painted the Linley sisters, the artist painted another portrait of his daughters (fig. 35), an unusually finished painting which was probably displayed prominently in his 'shew' room at Schomberg House, the family's London residence on Pall Mall.[6] The two portraits share much in their composition and setting, but subtle differentiations in posture and attitude convey the unique dynamics between each pair of sisters. Mary Linley engages the viewer from her seated position with a confiding half-smile, while her sister Elizabeth gazes wistfully out to the left, lost in reverie. This careful balance again recalls Van Dyck's *Stuart Brothers*, standing on their upper and lower steps, reserved and assertive in turn. By contrast, the Gainsborough sisters stand side by side, Margaret turned towards Mary, Mary's arm around Margaret's shoulders. This highly formal portrait presents the artist's daughters as fashionable society women, an image that Margaret and Mary wished to cultivate as they entered London society and began 'husband hunting'.[7] Like their mother, the illegitimate daughter of the 3rd Duke of Bedford, both were proud of their aristocratic blood, and benefited from an annuity from their grandfather's family.[8] Their closeness is emphasised by their dog, a symbol of fidelity often reserved for marriage portraits. This white English water spaniel may be the Gainsborough family's pet dog Tristram, who was also once included in *The Blue Boy*, now painted over and only visible in the painting's X-radiograph.[9] IT

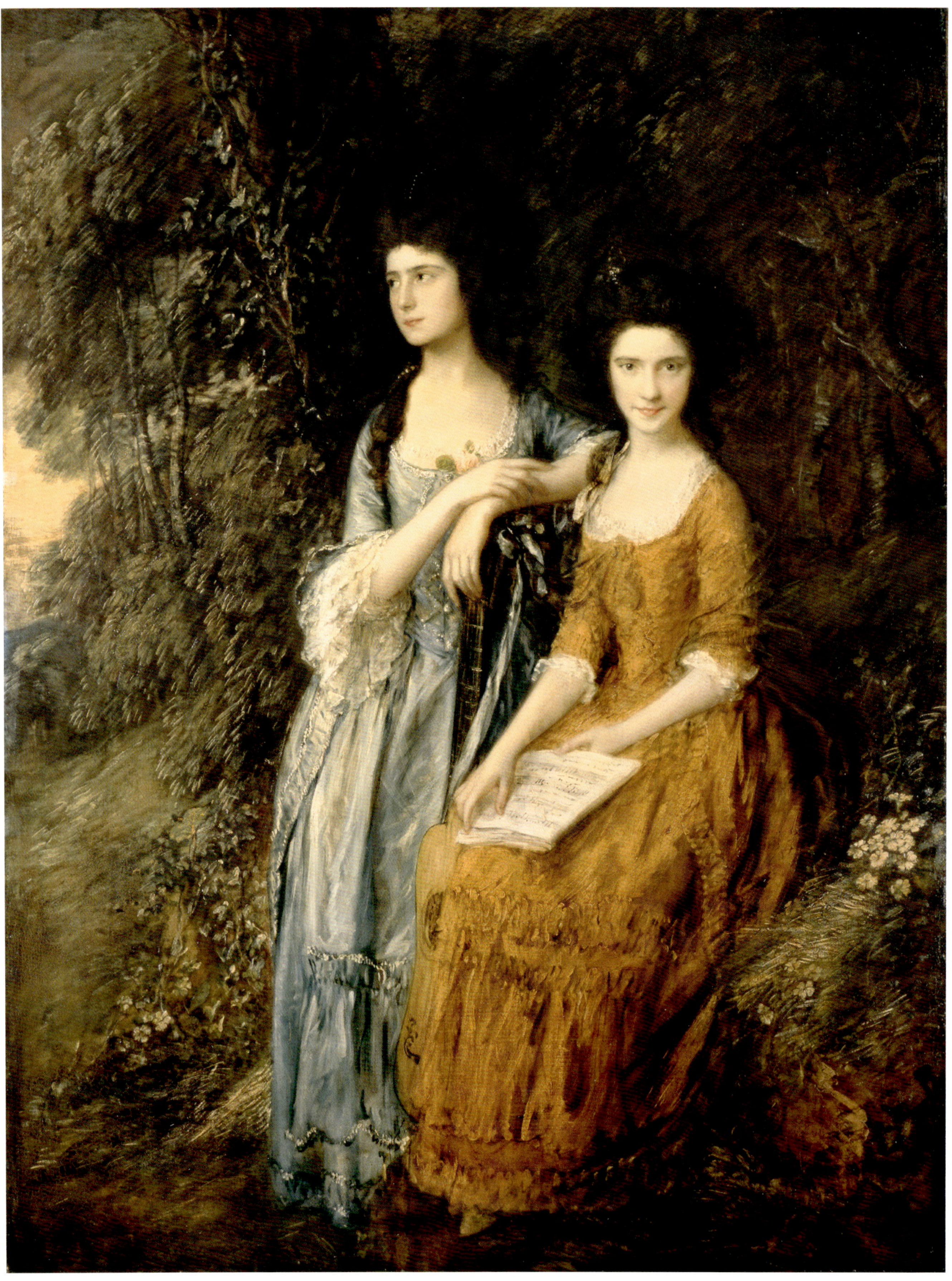

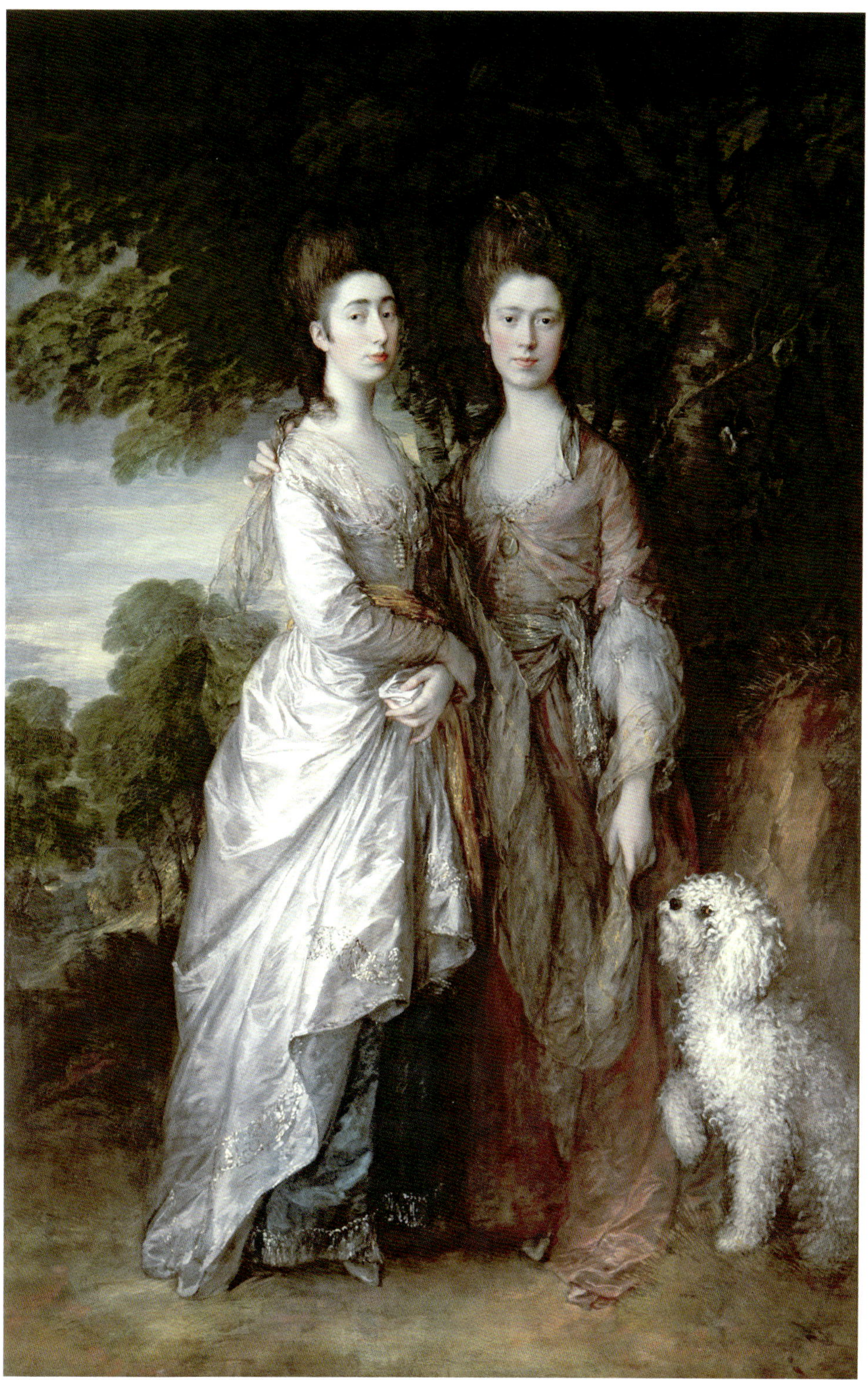

Fig. 35
Thomas Gainsborough (1727–1788)
Mary and Margaret Gainsborough, the Artist's Daughters, about 1774
Oil on canvas, 248.7 × 150 cm
Private collection

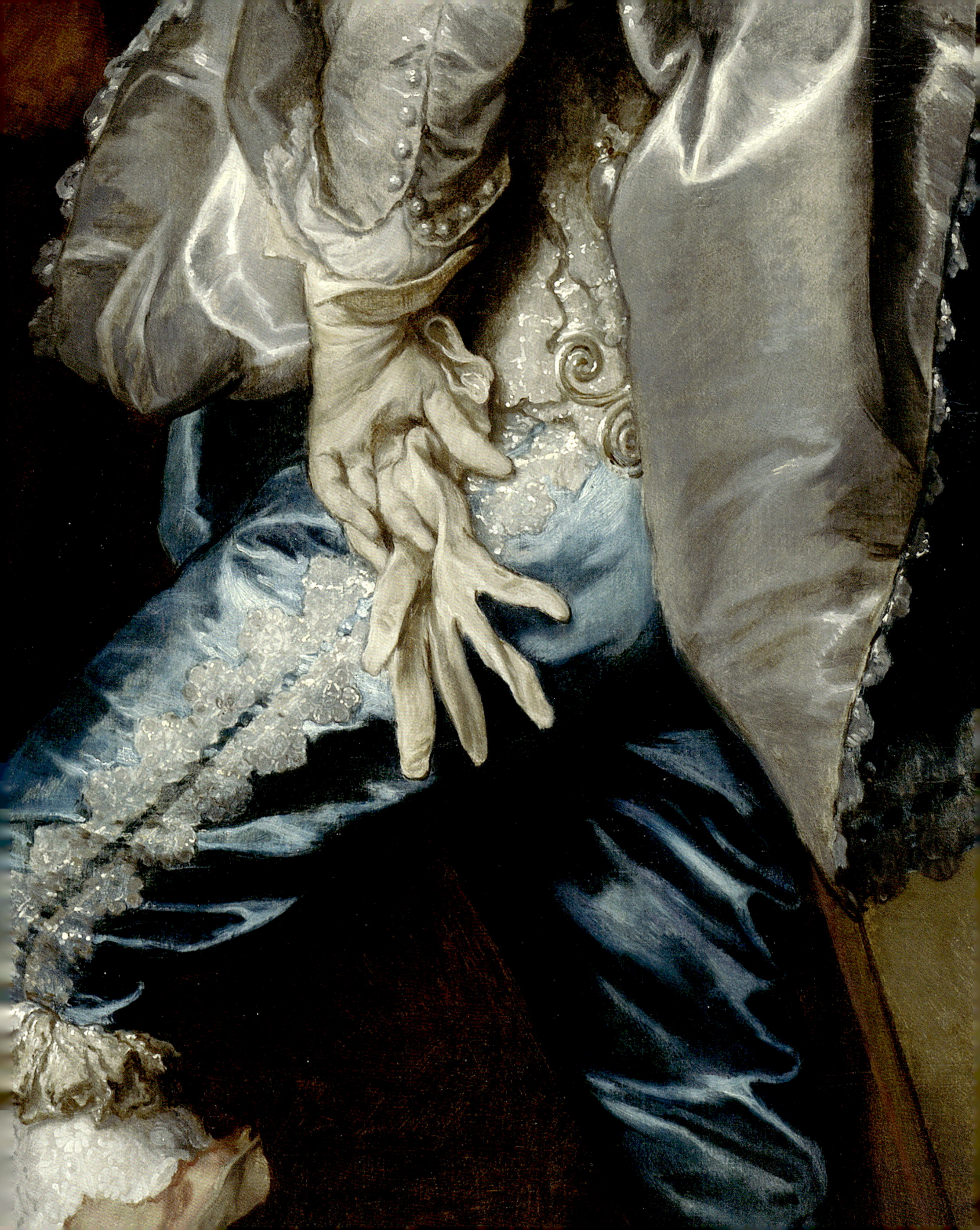

4
Anthony van Dyck (1599–1641)

Lord John Stuart and his Brother, Lord Bernard Stuart, about 1638

Oil on canvas, 237.5 × 146.1 cm
The National Gallery, London (NG6518)

Lords John (1621–1644) and Bernard Stuart (1623–1645) were the younger sons of the 3rd Duke of Lennox, brothers to the 1st Duke of Richmond and 4th Duke of Lennox, and cousins to Charles I. Van Dyck painted both brothers on several occasions, but this portrait was perhaps painted as a remembrance before they left for a tour of the Continent in 1639. The brothers were both killed during the Civil War (1642–51), fighting for the Royalists.[1]

John, the elder brother, wearing golden satin, lolls on the upper step and gazes meditatively past his younger brother. Bernard is rather more assertive in his challenging stare, captured with one heeled boot stepping up towards his senior. He turns his blue cloak over his shoulder, drawing attention to its fabulous silver satin lining, which matches a shimmering silver sleeve. The stance is borrowed from Correggio's *Madonna and Child with Saint George* (around 1530, Gemäldegalerie Alte Meister, Dresden).[2] Van Dyck had used a similar combination of frontal and three-quarter profile gazes in other 'friendship portraits', such as the *Portrait of the Princes Palatine* (1637, Musée du Louvre, Paris), but *The Stuart Brothers* represent a unique achievement in conveying character and relationship through stance and attitude. The portrait is perfectly balanced and yet charged with tension, as the younger brother's entitled energy jostles for precedence with the louche nonchalance of his senior.

The Stuart Brothers made a great impression on Gainsborough. He made an accurate copy of the painting (fig. 5), probably on site at Cobham Hall in the 1760s.[3] In 1765 he was commissioned to paint a portrait of the owner's niece, Theodosia Magill, later Countess of Clanwilliam.[4] The Earl of Darnley, who owned the original Van Dyck double portrait, purchased Gainsborough's copy at the sale of his works in 1789. Gainsborough had a reputation for copying Van Dyck's paintings with great accuracy, and indeed Reynolds remarked that even the most skilled connoisseur might mistake Gainsborough's copies after Van Dyck for the original.[5]

The shining satin doublets and neatly frilled collars of Van Dyck dress were a popular costume of choice for sitters in the eighteenth century, and *The Stuart Brothers*' luxurious textiles were undoubtedly part of the painting's appeal to Gainsborough, who was interested in Van Dyck's representation of brilliant silks and satins. However, art theorist Jonathan Richardson, whose opinion Gainsborough respected, considered Van Dyck's greatest achievement to be his ability to capture accurate and sincere likenesses.[6] Gainsborough was particularly interested in the psychological intrigue implied by the contrasting directions of the brothers' gaze, as well as the painting's balance of colours and interrelated, complementary stances. He worked through these ideas in double portraits such as *Elizabeth and Mary Linley* (cat. 3) and *Portrait of the Artist's Daughters* (fig. 36). Painted in Bath, when the girls were about 12 and 14, this portrait suggests an early preoccupation with *The Stuart Brothers*. An X-ray of the latter portrait reveals that Gainsborough originally intended to position Margaret in the upper left of the canvas, facing her older, seated sister, a composition even closer to Van Dyck's painting than the double portrait of the Linley sisters.[7] Standing behind Mary in the finished composition, Margaret rests her left arm behind her sister in a posture that echoes John Stuart's nonchalant lean on a column. Even her deep-blue satin sleeve swathes her arm in an echo of Van Dyck's elegant youth. IT

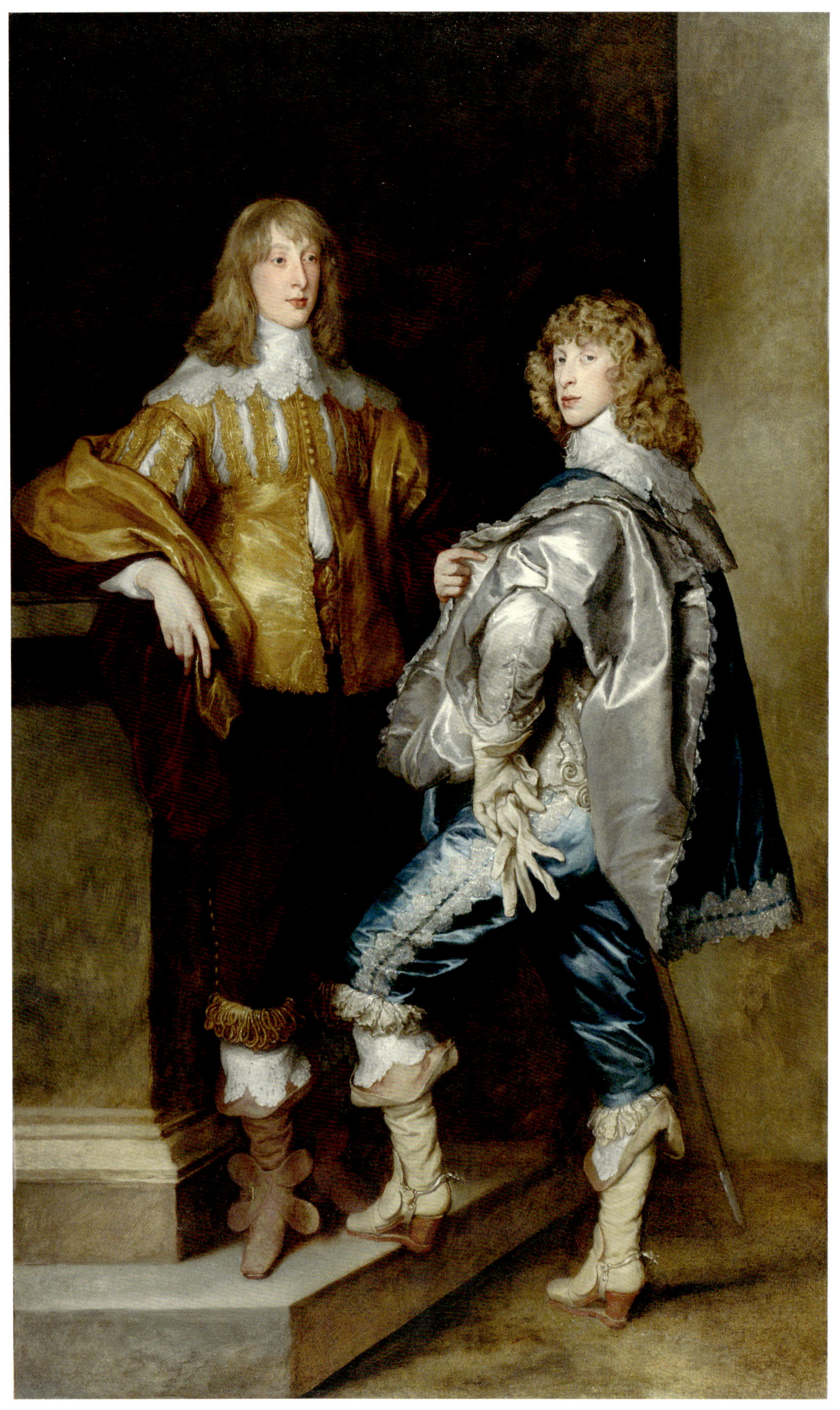

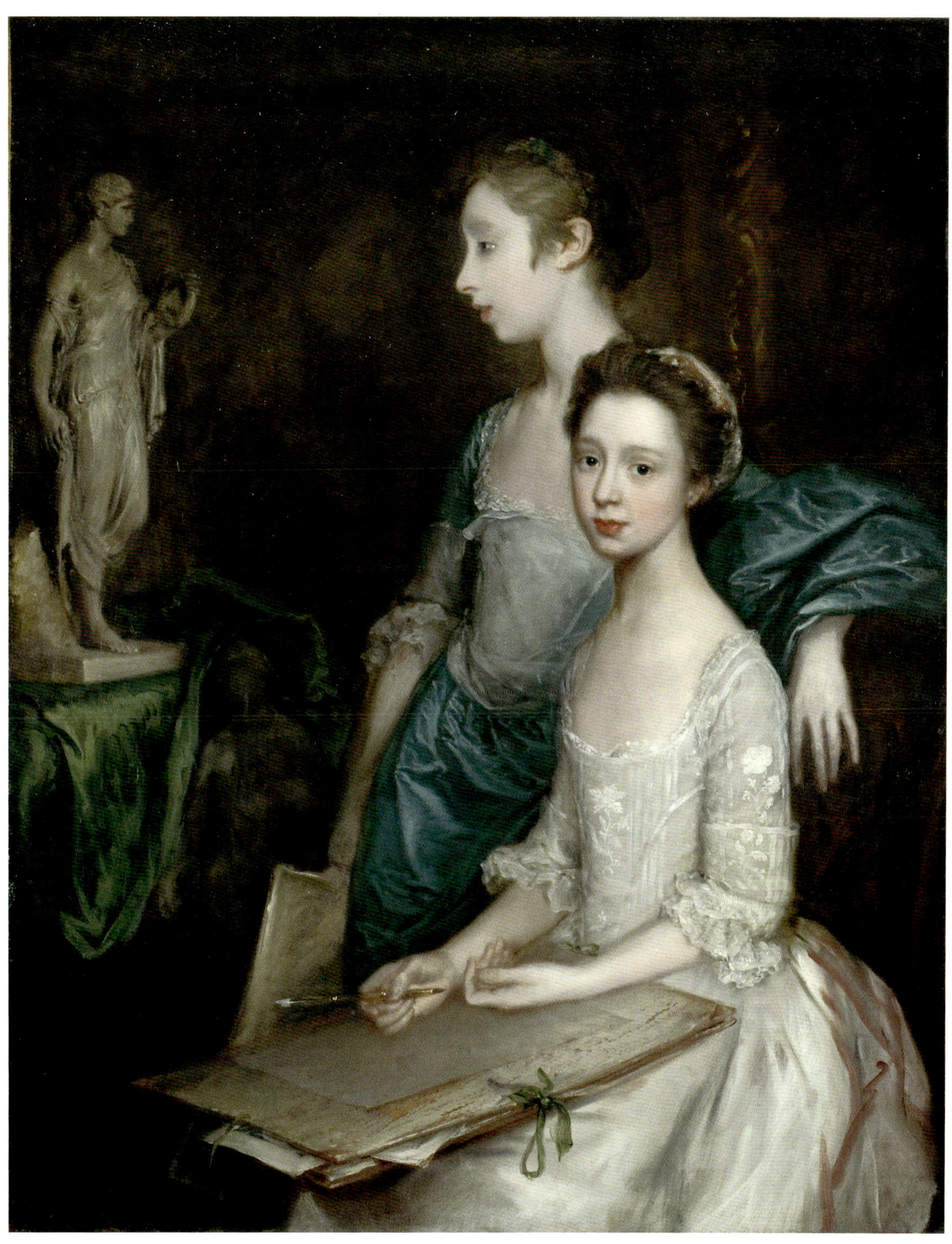

Fig. 36
Thomas Gainsborough (1727–1788)
Portrait of the Artist's Daughters, about 1763–4
Oil on canvas, 127.3 × 101.7 cm
Worcester Art Museum, Worcester, MA

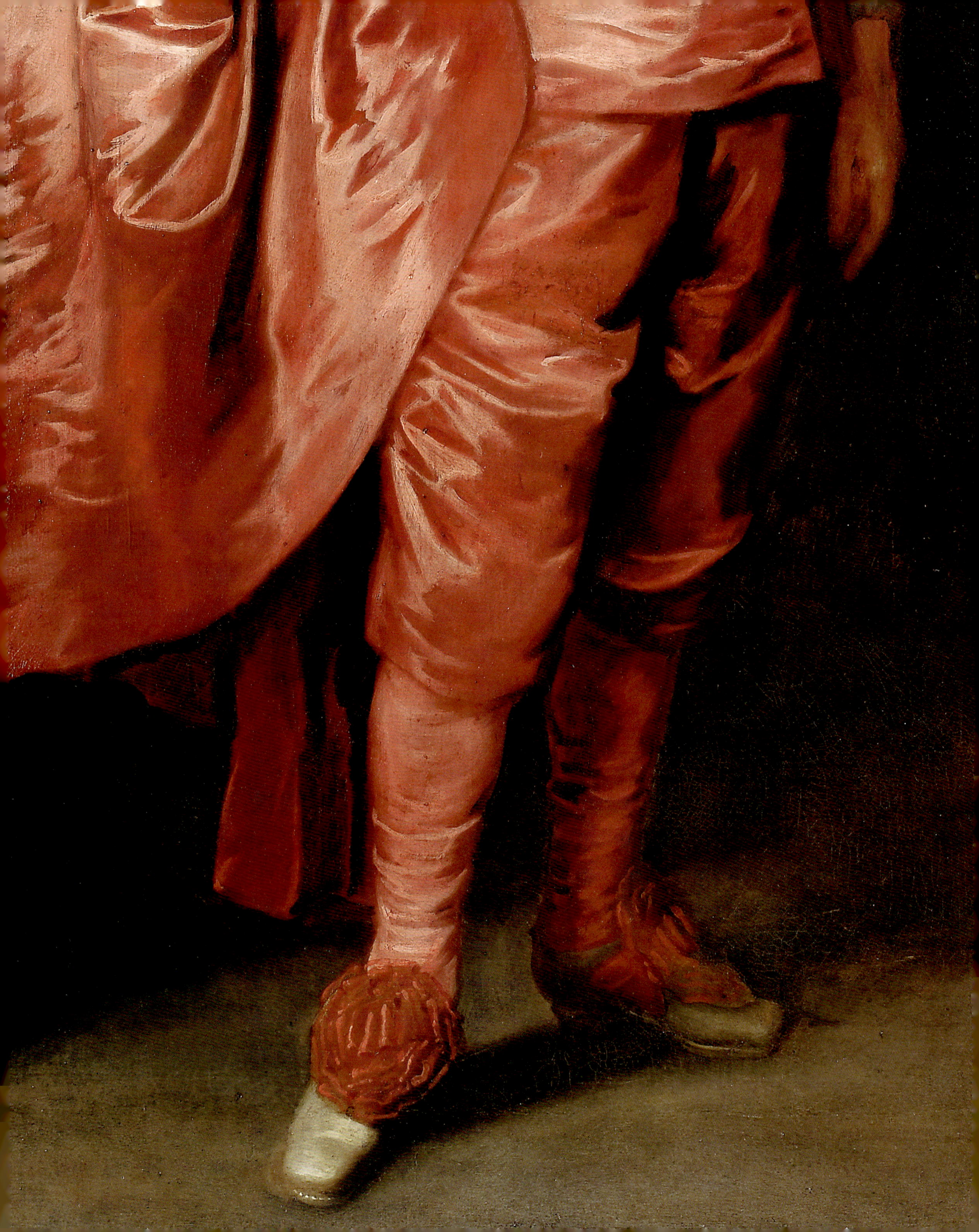

5

Anthony van Dyck (1599–1641)

George Villiers, 2nd Duke of Buckingham (1628–1687) and Lord Francis Villiers (1629–1648), 1635

Oil on canvas, 137.2 × 127.7 cm
The Royal Collection / HM Queen Elizabeth II
(RCIN 404401)

This double portrait of George Villiers (1628–1687), 2nd Duke of Buckingham, and his younger brother, Lord Francis Villiers (1629–1648), was commissioned by Charles I, who brought up the young Villiers boys with his own children at Richmond Palace after the murder of their father, the 1st Duke of Buckingham, in 1628.[1] The brothers were put into the care of Algernon Percy, Earl of Northumberland, and sent on a tour of the Continent in 1646 before returning to fight in the Civil War. Lord Francis lost his life in the Battle of Surbiton, near Kingston-upon-Thames, Surrey, in 1648. George went on to join Charles II's court in exile, later marrying the daughter of Thomas, Lord Fairfax (1612–1671), a parliamentarian.

When Van Dyck came to paint this double portrait, the Villiers boys had previously sat for him for a group portrait with their sister and widowed mother.[2] Portraits of children had been a particular specialism of Van Dyck's since his time in Genoa (1621–7). Here the boys' full-length stance invests them with the stature and solemnity of miniature adults, swaggering yet vulnerable, swathed in lusciously crumpled satins. George, the elder brother, stands slightly ahead of the younger Francis, who looks at George to echo his assured stance of hand on rose-clad hip with a less assertive gesture of his own, one gloved hand pulling his swathes of golden fabric to his chest protectively. The boys stand in rather a sombre setting, with a dark curtain and a brooding landscape visible through the window to the right. There is an original addition of over 7 cm of canvas at the bottom of the painting, presumably added to include the elegant squared toe of the young Duke's rosetted boot.[3]

In 1771 Gainsborough borrowed George Villiers' pose for *The Blue Boy*, reversing his sway and hand on hip.[4] However, Gainsborough had been experimenting more loosely with the double portrait format offered by Van Dyck's picture as early as the 1750s, when he painted the first of six double portraits of his own daughters. *The Painter's Daughters chasing a Butterfly* (fig. 37) dates from the family's time in Ipswich, before they moved to Bath in the autumn of 1759.[5] The portrait is unfinished, by the standards of the time, and the brown ground shows through Margaret's dress as she reaches towards a thistle. Nonetheless it is a virtuosic experiment in conveying figures in motion, a sense captured through the movement of textiles, as the girls' muslin dresses shimmer in the changing light. These concerns would go on to inspire Gainsborough's lifelong study of Van Dyck's luxurious fabrics. By the mid-eighteenth century, the portrait of the Villiers boys probably hung near Van Dyck's contemporary *Five Eldest Children of Charles I* (fig. 2); Johan Joseph Zoffany included both paintings in his portrait of George III's eldest sons in 1765.[6] Several copies of the painting survive at Warwick Castle, Highclere Castle and Serlby Hall; the original, then held at Buckingham House, was engraved in mezzotint by James McArdell (around 1729–1765) in 1752.[7] In the second half of the eighteenth century, Van Dyck's representations of children became exemplars for British artists such as Hogarth and Reynolds as well as Gainsborough, whose paintings of children interacted with contemporary discourses that reimagined childhood as a time of innocence and play.[8] IT

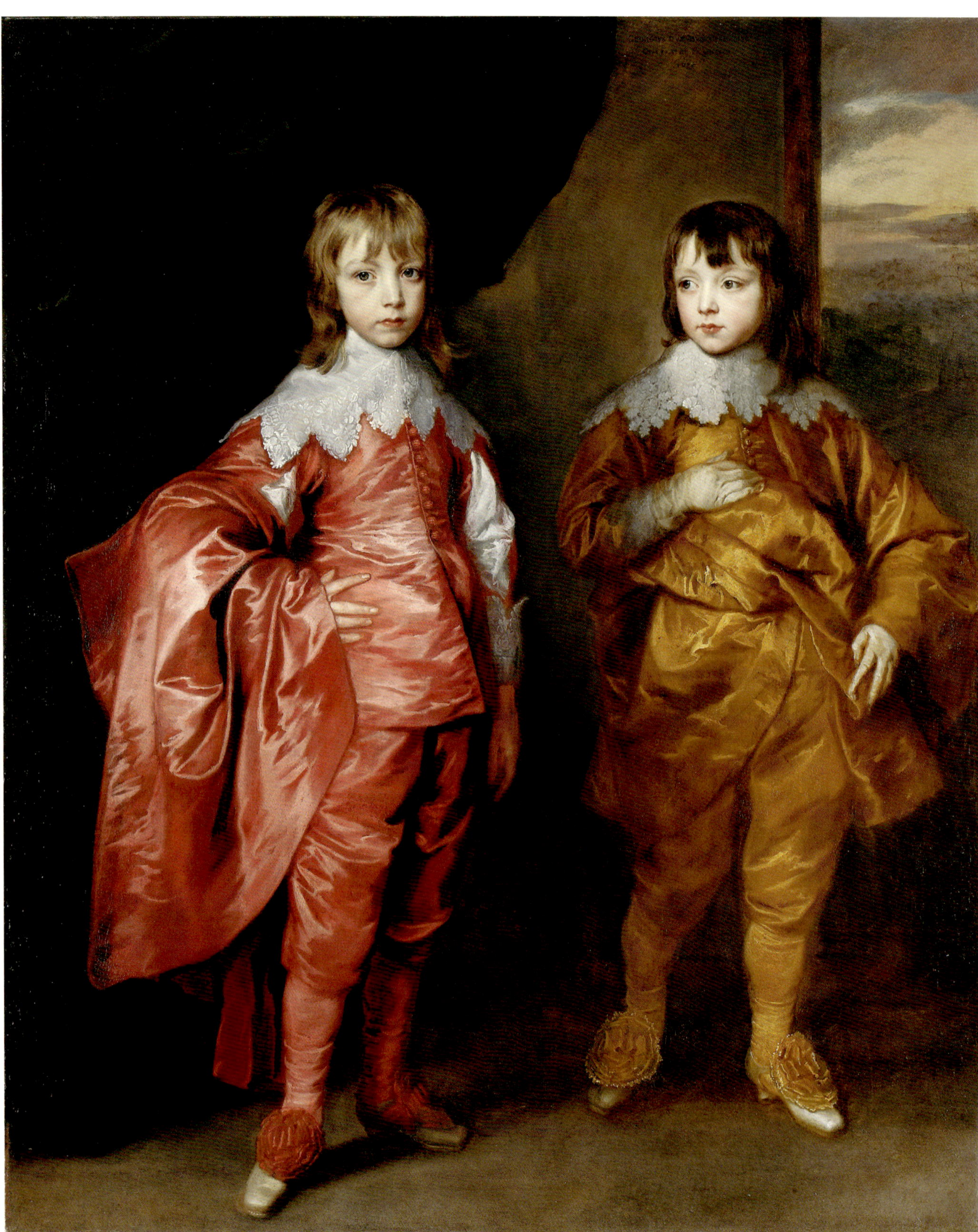

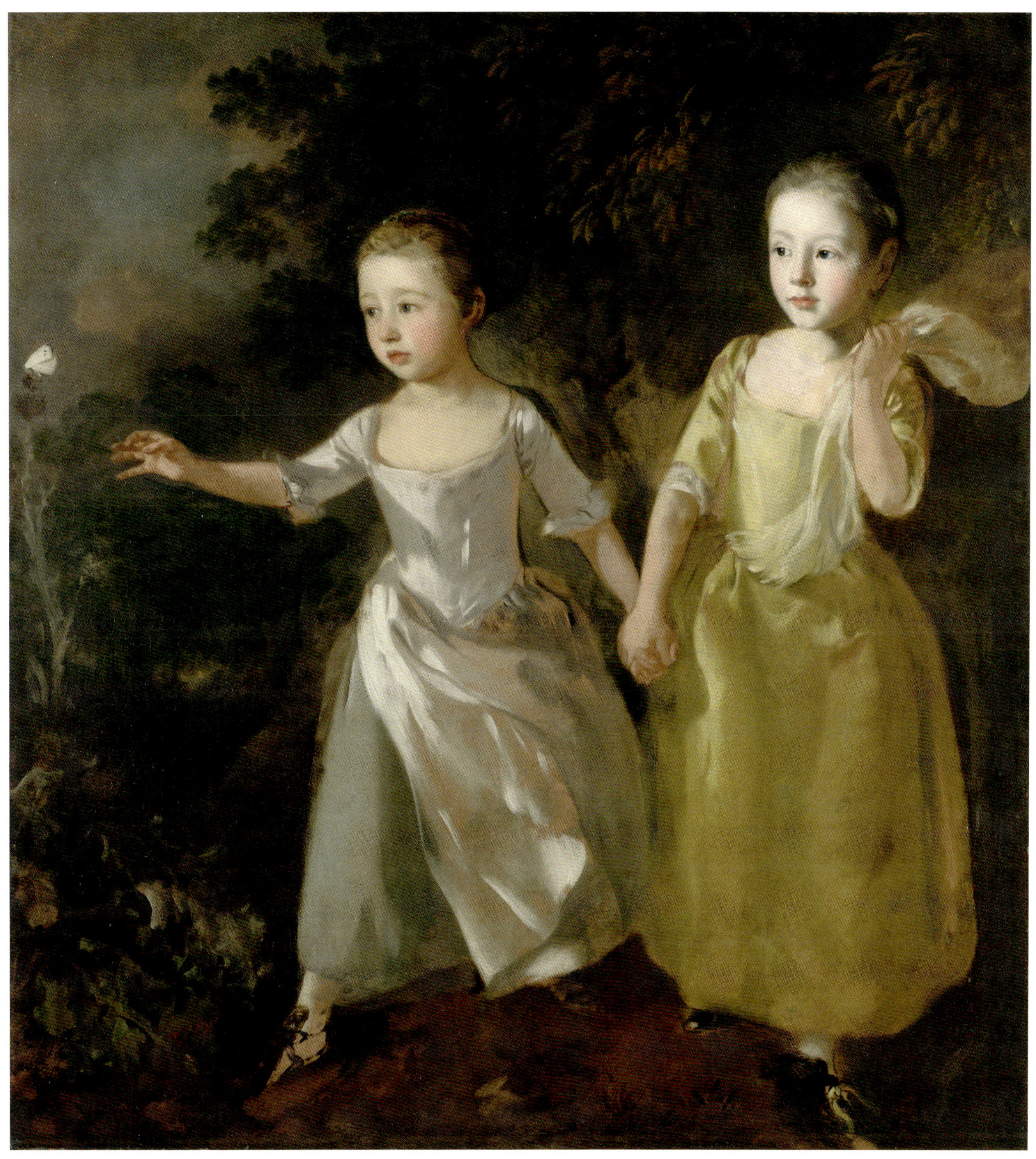

Fig. 37
Thomas Gainsborough (1727–1788)
The Painter's Daughters chasing a Butterfly,
about 1756
Oil on canvas, 113.5 × 105 cm
The National Gallery, London

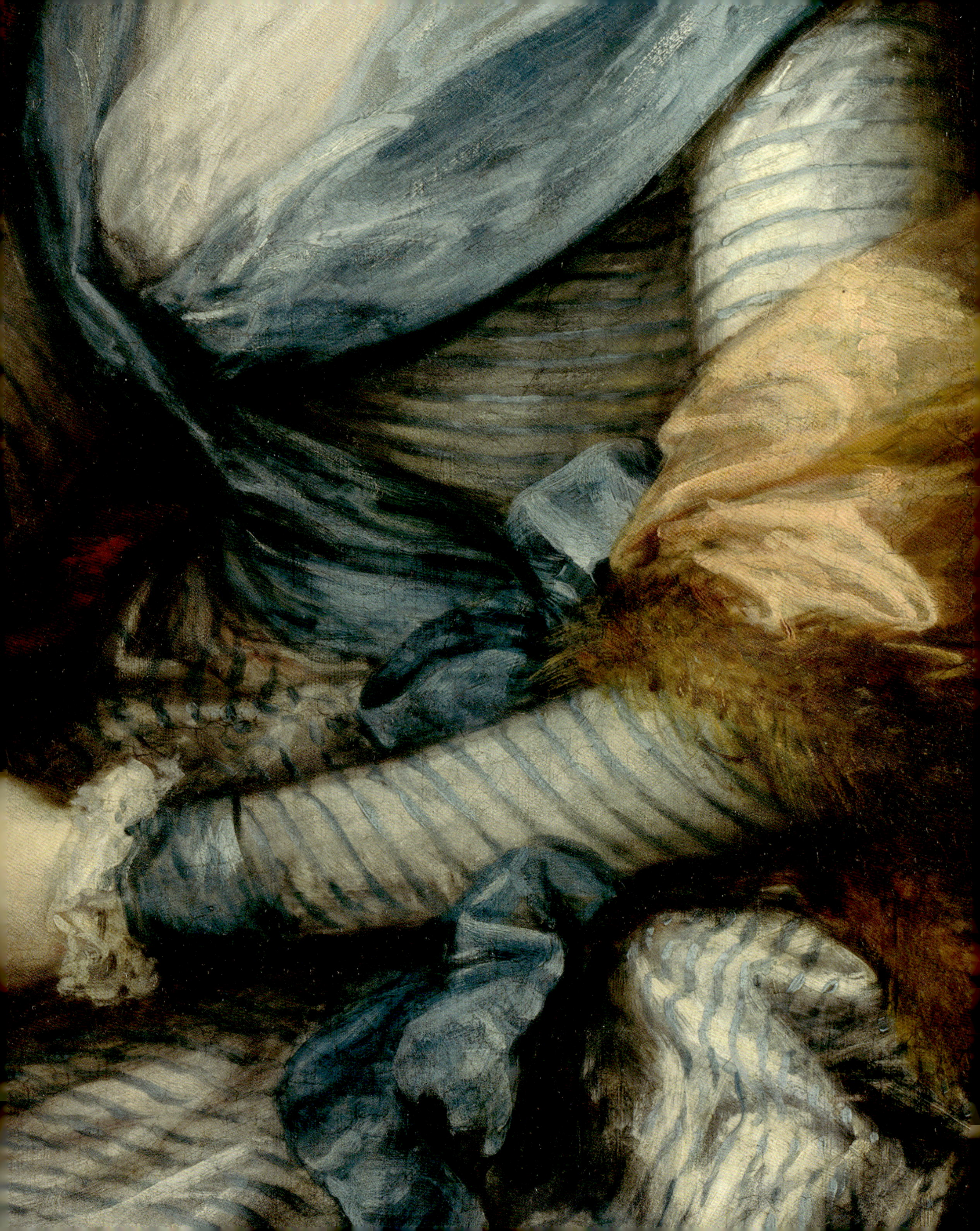

6

Thomas Gainsborough (1727–1788)

Mrs Siddons, 1785

Oil on canvas, 126 × 99.5 cm
The National Gallery, London (NG683)

Mrs Sarah Siddons (1755–1831) was the leading tragic actress of her age. The daughter of actors Roger and Sarah Kemble, she became the star attraction of Drury Lane Theatre, beginning with spectacularly successful runs in *Isabella* and *The Grecian Daughter* in 1782 and 1783, before debuting as Lady Macbeth to great acclaim in 1785. From spring 1783, she was appointed Reader in English to the royal children.[1] Even before performing Lady Macbeth, Siddons had become an embodiment of Tragedy. Sir Joshua Reynolds's painting *Sarah Siddons as the Tragic Muse* (fig. 38) was exhibited at the Royal Academy in 1784, perhaps inspired by William Russell's 'The Tragic Muse: A Poem addressed to Mrs Siddons', published in early 1783.[2]

Siddons had little patience with portrait sittings, considering them a distraction from her work as an actress and her responsibilities to her family.[3] She may have sat for Gainsborough only once, and the artist took great care in capturing her likeness in black chalk on that occasion.[4] Siddons debuted as Lady Macbeth on 2 February 1785, and the *Morning Herald* reported that the portrait was 'nearly finished' on 12 March, so the painting was almost certainly painted while she was performing this most famous of her roles. Thomas Beach's contemporary portrait of Siddons and John Philip Kemble as Lady Macbeth and Macbeth (1786, Garrick Club, London) shows her wearing the Van Dyck dress that was then commonly worn to perform Shakespeare, together with a large black hat not dissimilar to that in Gainsborough's portrait.

Unlike Reynolds, Beach and other contemporaries, Gainsborough declines to paint Siddons in character or in costume. Instead, he presents an intimate, refined likeness of Siddons as a professional woman. Her fashionable pale blue striped 'wrapper-dress' – a practical garment for a busy working mother and actress – is the latest fashion, worn with a golden silk mantle edged with fox fur, choker, and the large black hat at a jaunty angle.[5] The painting's surface is highly finished and heavily worked for Gainsborough. Cross-sections of the paint layers show complex paint structures, particularly in Siddons's dress and the red curtain that hangs behind the sitter. This swag of dark fabric is less common in the work of Gainsborough than in that of his predecessors Van Dyck and Rubens, as the French critic Théophile Thoré-Bürger observed when he saw the portrait at the Manchester Art Treasures exhibition in 1857; preferring *Mrs Siddons* to *The Blue Boy*, which hung nearby, the critic declared that the former deserved a place in the Louvre.[6] The curtain invests Siddons with theatricality, as does the magnificently feathered hat that bears a striking resemblance to her Lady Macbeth costume. Though her gaze remains resolute and dignified, the portrait is animated by the lively patterns, colourful fabrics and rustling textures of her splendid attire.

Gainsborough's portrait was not exhibited at the Royal Academy but instead displayed in the artist's studio at Schomberg House for at least a year. Nonetheless, comparison with Reynolds's portrait was unavoidable, if favourable. Henry Bate-Dudley was not alone in his observation that Gainsborough had avoided 'that *theatrical distortion* which several painters have been fond of delineating'.[7] Since then, the portraits have been seen as emblematic of the artists' differing approaches to their work: Reynolds's pursuit of an intellectual and heroic art, and Gainsborough's of a social, private and natural art.[8] Certainly, the two paintings form part of a longer conversation between the artists, and Reynolds's contemporary portrait of Lady Catherine Cornewall (about 1785–6, National Gallery of Art, Washington DC) may borrow from Gainsborough's portrait of Siddons in its composition.[9] However, the two portraits have been seen together only once in their history, when Reynolds's painting was lent to the National Gallery together with *The Blue Boy* in 1922, before both pictures departed Britain, bound for California. IT

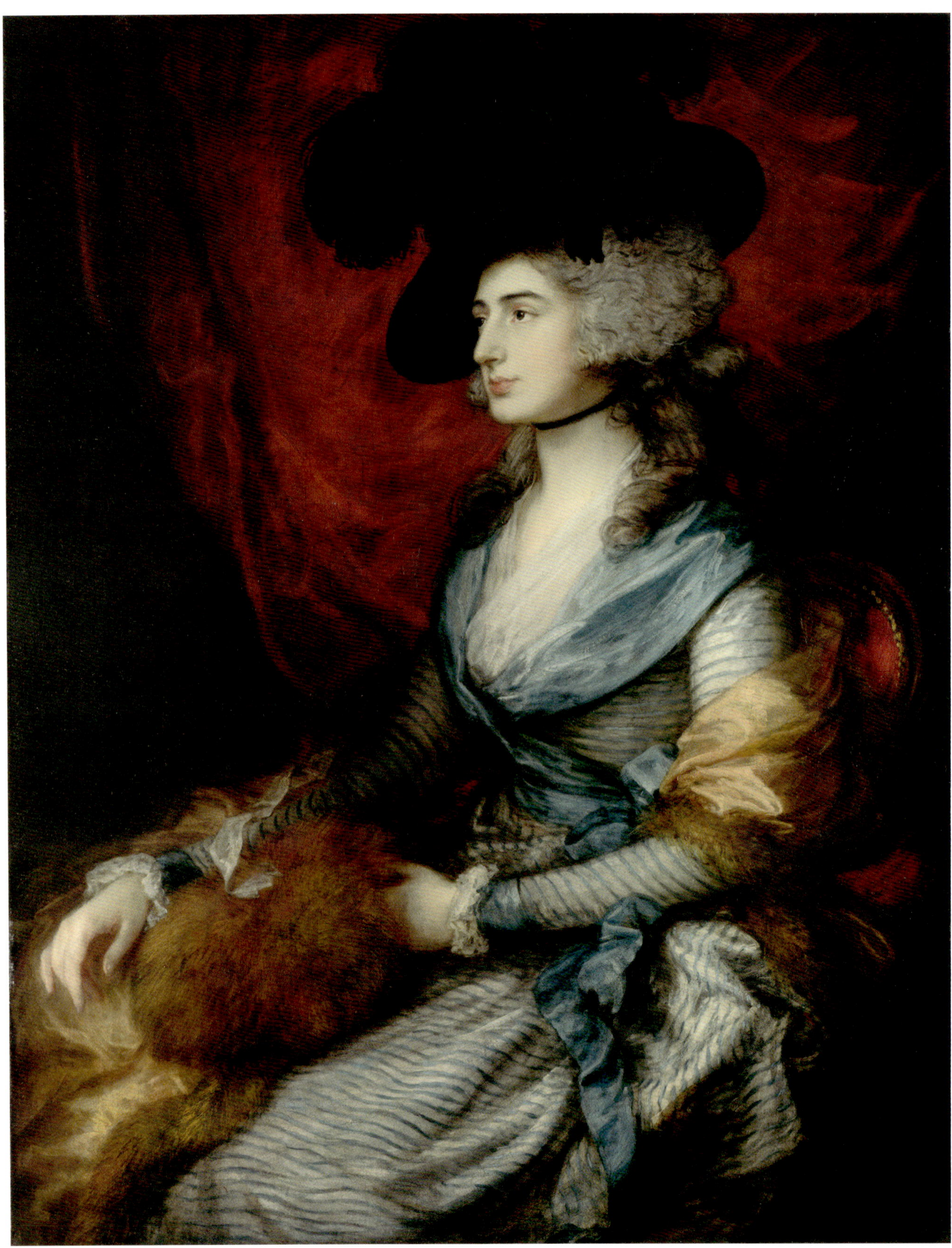

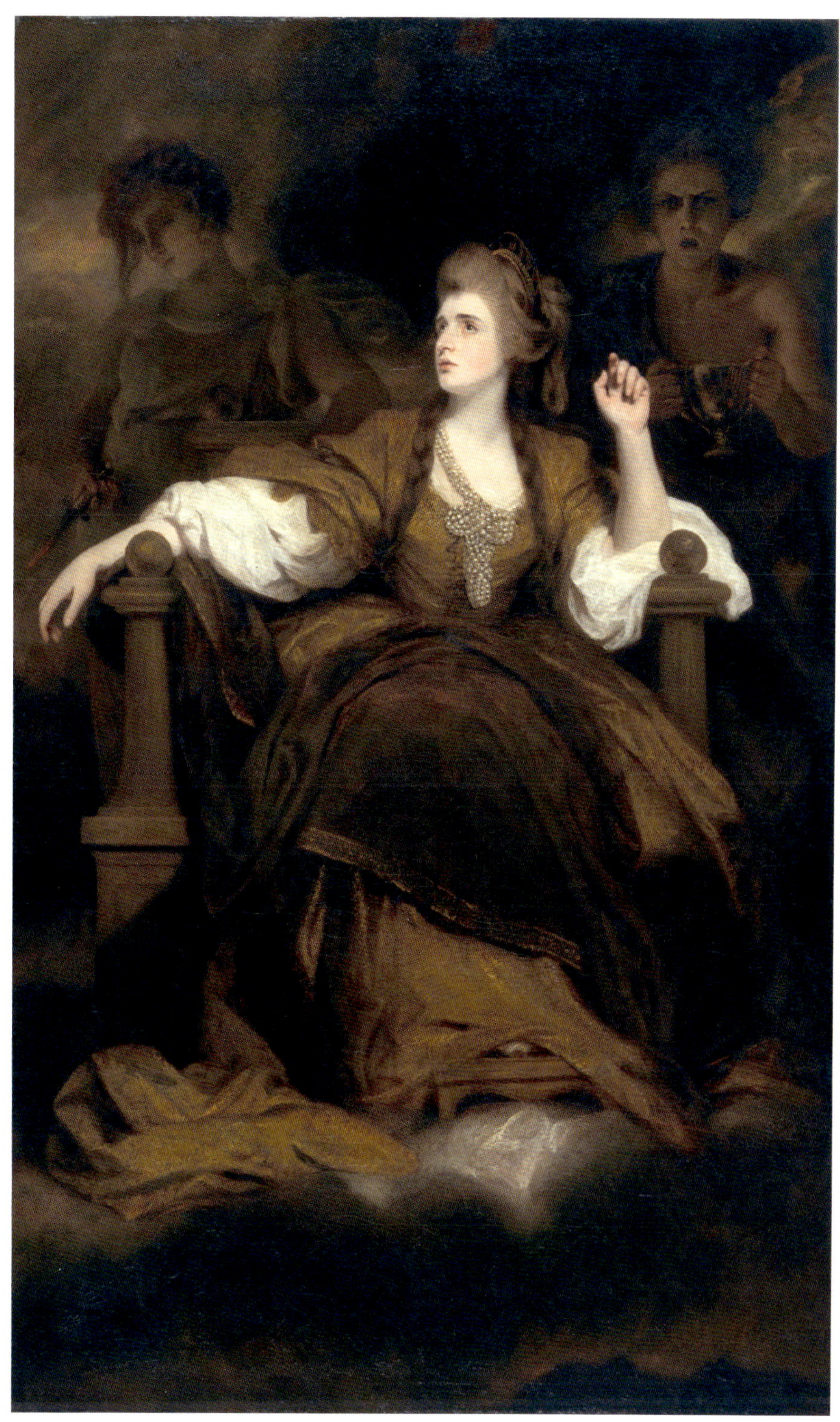

Fig. 38
Sir Joshua Reynolds (1723–1792)
Sarah Siddons as the Tragic Muse, 1783–4
Oil on canvas, 239.4 × 147.6 cm
The Huntington Library, Art Museum, and Botanical Gardens, San Marino, California

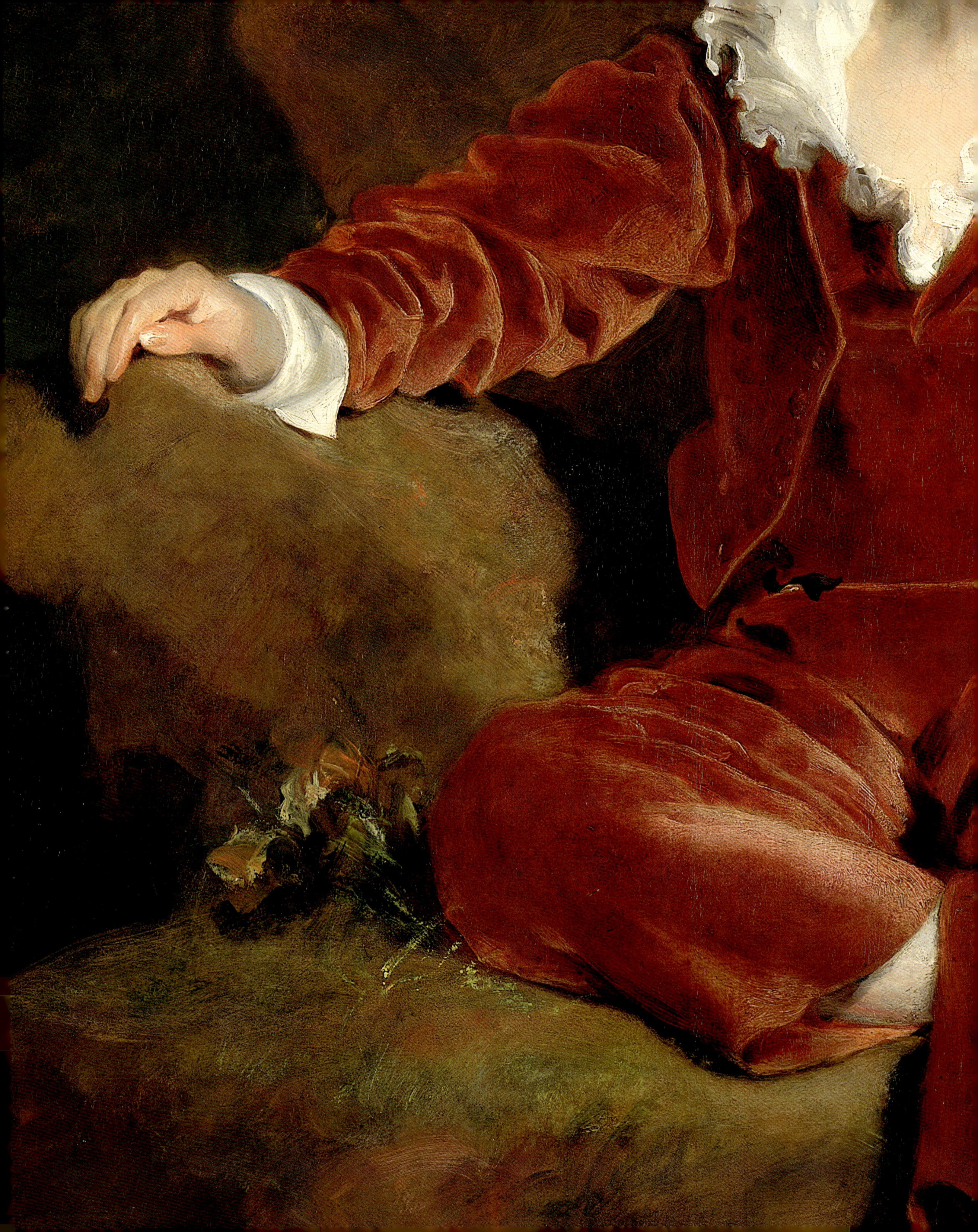

7
Sir Thomas Lawrence (1769–1830)
Portrait of Charles William Lambton ('The Red Boy'), 1825

Oil on canvas, 137.2 × 111.8 cm
The National Gallery, London (NG6692)

This portrait of Charles William Lambton, aged six or seven, was commissioned by the sitter's father John George Lambton, Whig politician and MP for County Durham. Seated on a rocky promontory overlooking the moonlit sea, Lambton is styled as a youthful Byronic wanderer, lost in contemplation of the sublime. The painting may be inspired by William Wordsworth's poem 'There was a Boy' (1798) or allude to one of the artist's own poems addressed to a boy climbing a rock.[1] With his fragile youth symbolised by the blooming flowers at his side, the sitter is presented on the cusp of a journey through life, though he later died of tuberculosis aged only thirteen.

Like Gainsborough, Lawrence had an avid interest in the work of his predecessors, attested by his extraordinary collection of old master drawings and his involvement in the foundation of the National Gallery in 1824.[2] From early in his career, Lawrence emulated the closeness between Gainsborough and his royal patrons. His early portrait of Queen Charlotte (1789, National Gallery, London) was not acquired by the sitter, who disliked the picture, and so it did not join Gainsborough's earlier portrait of the queen (about 1781, Royal Collection).[3] However in 1792, Lawrence was made Painter in Ordinary to King George III, and, with his knighthood in 1815 and appointment as President of the Royal Academy from 1820, he went on to become the unchallenged heir to Gainsborough, Reynolds and indeed Van Dyck.

Lawrence's response to Gainsborough's achievements is attested by his portraits of children and young adults, for which he acquired an unparalleled reputation. His arresting 'coming of age' portrait of Arthur Atherley (fig. 10), exhibited in 1792 as *Portrait of an Etonian*, garnered admiring comments from the critics. Although he wears contemporary dress, Atherley's gaze and pose draw parallels with *The Blue Boy* and Van Dyck's *Stuart Brothers*.[4] Three years later, he exhibited a portrait of 11-year-old Sarah Goodin Barrett Moulton (fig. 39). With its low horizon line, grandiose scale and focus on its young subject, this portrait constitutes a bold response to *The Blue Boy*. It was commissioned by the sitter's grandmother, who wrote from the family home in St James, Jamaica, asking for a portrait 'in an easy, careless attitude'.[5] Like Master Lambton, Miss Barrett did not survive childhood, and died the day before her portrait went on display at the Royal Academy. The iridescent sheen of her muslin dress, swirling around her elongated body, together with her shining pink sash, bonnet and ribbons wafting in the breeze, seem to allude to the sitter's family nickname: 'Pinkie'. The painting was known by this sobriquet in 1927, when, like *The Blue Boy*, it was purchased by financier Henry E. Huntington from Joseph Duveen, for the unprecedented sum of $380,000, following its exhibition at the Royal Society of Portrait Painters.[6] As a result, '*Pinkie*' and *The Blue Boy* have hung together in California for nearly a century.

After the sale of *The Blue Boy* in 1922, the *Illustrated London News* published reproductions of 'Sir Thomas Lawrence's equally charming portrait which we have named "The Red Boy"'.[7] Ten years later, Duveen emphasised this connection in his attempts to sell 'The Red Boy' at auction, though the painting failed to reach its reserve of £100,000.[8] Lawrence's portrait received increasing attention thanks to a popular story that Master Lambton had originally been painted wearing yellow.[9] In fact, Master Lambton's striking outfit is by no means unique among Lawrence's child portraits, in which several of his young subjects wear similar red velvet 'skeleton suits'.[10] By 1800, these suits had become popular among elite families, replacing Van Dyck dress as a costume aiding greater freedom of movement and outdoor play.[11] IT

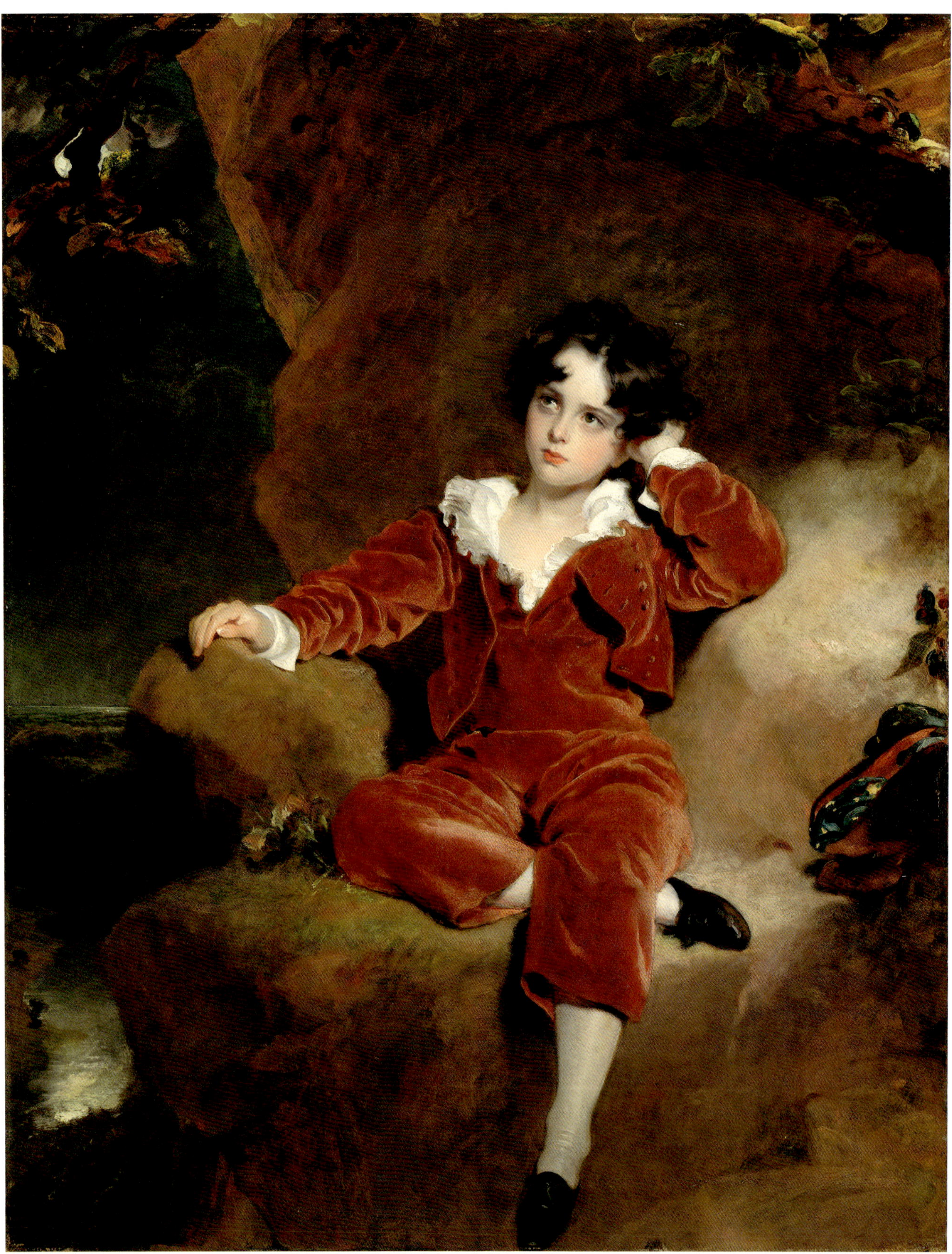

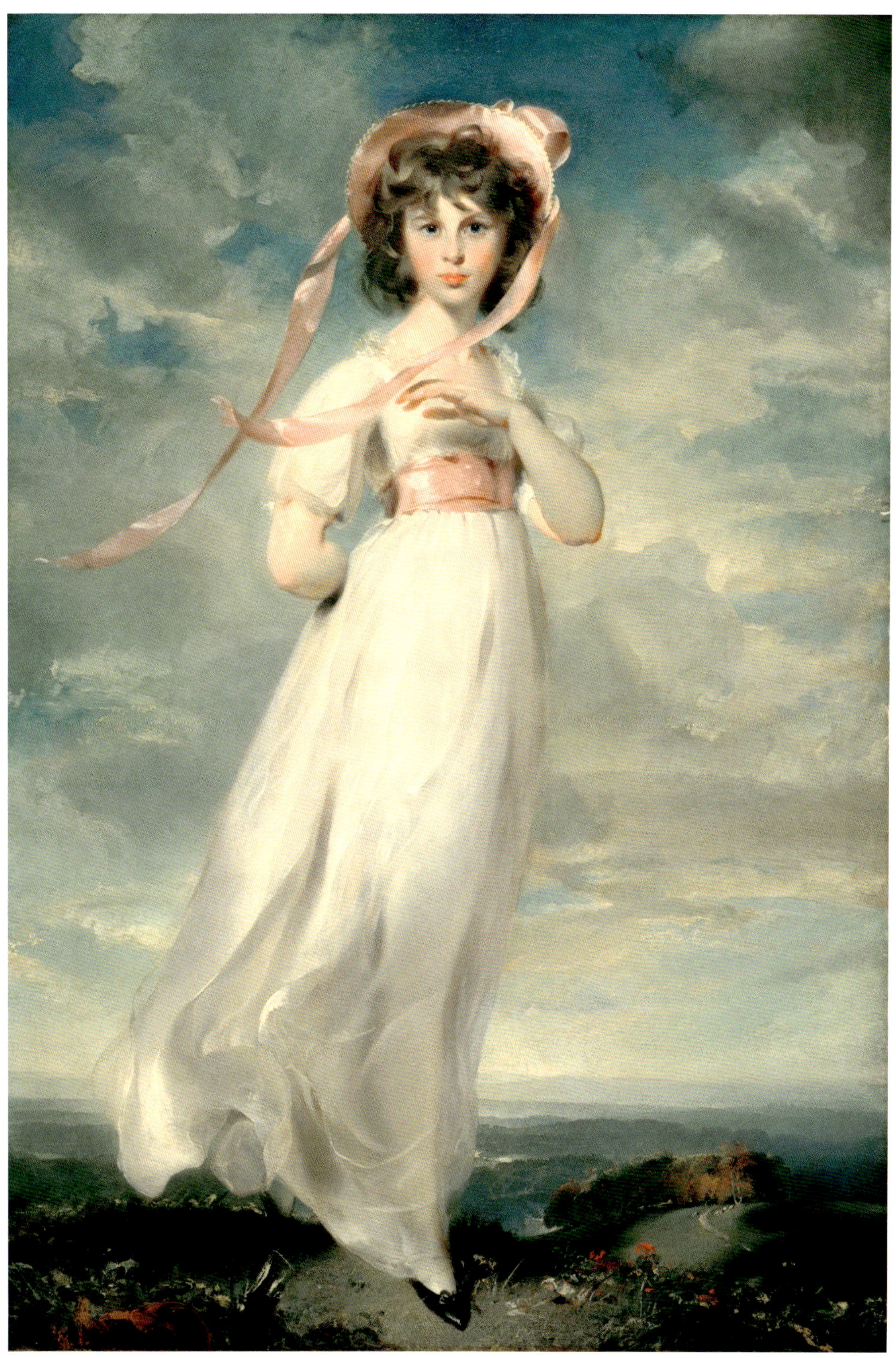

Fig. 39
Sir Thomas Lawrence (1769–1830)
Sarah Goodin Barrett Moulton: 'Pinkie', 1794
Oil on canvas, 148 × 102.2 cm
The Huntington Library, Art Museum, and
Botanical Gardens, San Marino, California

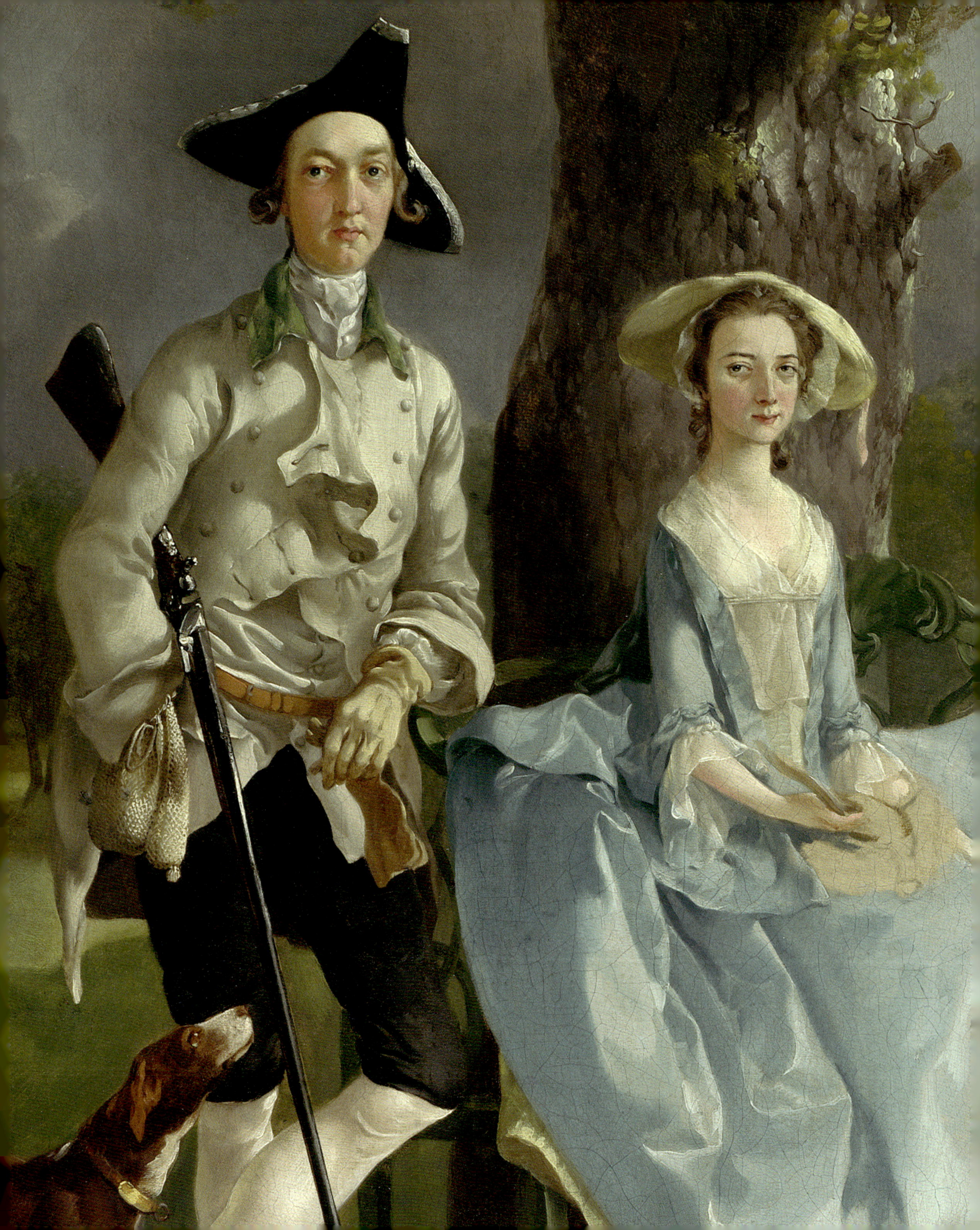

Notes

Van Dyck, Gainsborough and *The Blue Boy*

1 Desmond Shawe-Taylor, 'The Royal Portrait' in London 2018b, pp. 126–31; London 2009, p. 65.
2 London 2009, pp. 205–8.
3 Egerton 1998, p. 74.
4 Hayes 2001, p. 90.
5 Sloman 2002, pp. 51–4.
6 Mowl and Earnshaw 1988, pp. 69, 197.
7 Hart 2011, pp. 228–46.
8 Gainsborough's first, large-scale three-quarter-length commission was that of Admiral Edward Vernon in 1753 (private collection). See Belsey 2019, vol. 2, p. 843.
9 Hallet and Riding 2006, pp. 95–6; Riding 2017, pp. 33–4, 53–5, 57–83; Retford 2017, pp. 13–19, 22–4.
10 Egerton 1998, p. 80.
11 Ann Bermingham, 'Daughters and Sisters' in London 2018a, pp. 49–50.
12 Riding 2021, pp. 238–9; Burke 1955, p. 217.
13 Smart 1992, pp. 48, 78.
14 Einberg 2016, pp. 242–4, 292–4.
15 Ibid, p. 294. The portrait was probably commissioned for display at Daniel Graham's newly refurbished property on Pall Mall.
16 See for example Rosenthal 1999, pp. 23–4, and Sloman 2002, pp. 1–3, 5–8.
17 C. Gambarini, 'A Description of the Earl of Pembroke's Pictures', London 1731, pp. 3–11; Malcolm Rogers, 'Van Dyck in England' in London and Antwerp 1999, pp. 83–4.
18 For *The Lee Family* see Riding 2017, pp. 41–53, and for *The Marlborough Family* see Mannings 2000, cat. 1674, pp. 425–6.
19 The print series *Iconographie* was begun in the 1620s, and Van Dyck continued it while in London in the 1630s. The first known edition was published after the artist's death in 1645; see London 2009, pp. 134, 144–9.
20 Jonathan Yarker, 'Copies after Old Masters' in Belsey 2019, vol. 2, pp. 1001–8.
21 Van Dyck's portrait was then at Cobham Hall in the collection of Gainsborough's patron, John Bligh, 3rd Earl of Darnley.
22 Yarker in Belsey 2019, vol. 2, pp. 989–90.
23 Christine Riding, 'Robert Craggs', 'William Poyntz' and 'James Quin' in London 2002, pp. 94–101.
24 Riding in London 2002, pp. 100–1; Belsey 2019, vol. 2, pp. 702–5.
25 Postle 1995, p. 21.
26 Ibid., p. 222; London 2002, pp. 266–7.
27 London 2018a, p. 120.
28 Riding in London 2002, pp. 110–11; Belsey 2019 vol. 2, p. 746–8. One likely source for Gainsborough's *Countess of Sefton* is the celebrated portrait of 'Rubens's Wife' as it was then called (*Portrait of Hélène Fourment*, about 1630–2, Museu Calouste Gulbenkian, Lisbon, inv. 959), sometimes incorrectly ascribed to Van Dyck, which was often copied, engraved and utilised for masquerade dress and portraiture.
29 For 'Rubens's Wife' in British art see Ribeiro 1995, pp. 195–8; Riding 2012, vol. 1, pp. 102–7.
30 London 2002, p. 116; Liverpool, London and San Marino 2002, pp. 19–22, 106–8, 115–17.
31 London 2009, p. 155.
32 Ribeiro 1995, p. 195.
33 As an example, the *Middlesex Journal* noted, about Gainsborough's paintings at the Royal Academy in 1772, that 'his performances of this year will lose him none of that fame which he so justly acquired by his former productions'. Quoted in London 2002, p. 120.
34 London 2009, pp. 16–17.
35 Jeremy Wood, 'Connoisseurship at the Caroline Court' in London 2018b, pp. 30–5.
36 London and Rome 1996, p. 22.
37 London and Düsseldorf 2020, pp. 96–7.
38 London 2005, pp. 141, 258.
39 London 2002, pp. 88, 120, 122; Rosenthal 1999, pp. 183–6.
40 Postle 2011, pp. 205–6.
41 Hedquist 2020, pp. 23–6.
42 Riding 2016, pp. 277, 293.
43 London 2009, pp. 19–21.
44 Belsey 2019, vol. 1, pp. 163–5, 171–3, 379–81.
45 London 2010, pp. 98–100, 105–7.
46 Quoted in Belsey 2019 vol. 1, p. 281.
47 Ibid.
48 Reynolds 1992, p. 219.
49 Ibid.
50 Ibid., p. 202.
51 Belsey 2019, vol. 1, p. 281.
52 Ibid.
53 Reynolds 1992, p. 199.
54 Belsey 2019, vol. 1, pp. 410–12; pp. 93–5.
55 Riding 2004, pp. 83–5.
56 Maclaren Young et al. 1980, pp. 68–9, 127–8; MacDonald 1995, pp. 102–4.

Gainsborough and the Status of British Art

1 Reynolds 1992, p. 301.
2 Ibid., p. 302.
3 Quoted in Cunningham 1830, vol. 1, p. 353.
4 Reynolds 1992, p. 307.
5 Quoted in Vaughan 2002, p. 207.
6 As quoted in London 2003, p. 192.
7 Reynolds 1891, p. 327.
8 Quoted in Sloman 2013, p. 234.
9 According to Joseph Farington, Hoppner was 'passionately enamoured' of Gainsborough and emulated his work, especially in his 'fancy pictures' of rural children; see Hedquist 2020, p. 43.
10 For a complete list of exhibitions to which *The Blue Boy* was lent, see Belsey 2019, vol. 1, p. 280.
11 Whitley 1930, p. 286; Hedquist 2020, p. 50.
12 Letter dated 19 June 1859, as quoted and translated in 'The Correspondence of James McNeill Whistler', University of Glasgow, at https://www.whistlerarts.gla.ac.uk/correspondence/people/display/?cid=8050&nameid=Gainsborough_T&sr=0&rs=2&surname=gainsborough&first-name= (accessed 8 August 2021).
13 Anonymous, 'Works of the Old Masters and Deceased British Artists', *Art Journal* 32 (1870), p. 41. See also anonymous, 'Exhibition of Old Masters at the Royal Academy', *The Times*, 3 January 1870.
14 Bellhouse 1857, p. 17.
15 Ireland 1857, p. 59.
16 Jameson 1844, pp. 227, 230; Passavant 1836, pp. 147–58.
17 Waagen 1854, II, p. 161.

18 'The Duke of Westminster's Collection at Grosvenor House', *Connoisseur* 1 (December 1901), p. 210.
19 See Belsey 2019, vol. 1, p. 280; Hedquist 2020, chapters 3 and 4.
20 Quoted in Egerton 1998, p. 113.
21 This work had already been accepted as a gift in 1835 but it had been returned to the family just three months later, after a dispute arose over its legal ownership.
22 *Blackwood's Edinburgh Magazine* 40, no. 250 (August 1836), p. 211.
23 Quoted in Egerton 1998, p. 14.
24 Ibid., pp. 13–15.
25 Sir Joshua Reynolds quoted by William Vaughan, 'Gainsborough's modernity', in www.tate.org.uk/art/artists/thomas-gainsborough-199/gainsboroughs-modernity (aacessed 3 April 2021)
26 The pastels and prints exist today, but the painting, *The Blue Girl: Purple and Blue* (1872–6), was not completed. A fragment of it is in the Freer Gallery of Art, Washington (F1907.181a-c). Whistler returned to the 'Blue Girl' subject a few years later with *The Blue Girl: Connie Gilchrist* (about 1879, Hunterian Art Gallery, University of Glasgow, GLAHA_46320).
27 Way 1912, p. 30.
28 Gainsborough, *Lord Archibald Hamilton (1770–1827)*, 1786, Waddesdon Manor, Buckinghamshire.
29 Gainsborough, *Francis Nicholls, 'The Pink Boy'* (1782) and Highmore, *A Boy in Van Dyck Costume* (1748) both Waddesdon Manor, Buckinghamshire.
30 Hedquist 2020, p. 108, notes that in 1911, Arabella Huntington purchased from Duveen three Gainsborough portraits of Edward, Viscount Ligonier, his wife Penelope and Juliana, Baroness Petre.
31 Ormond and Kilmurray 2002, pp. 2–3.
32 www.npg.org.uk/collections/search/set/515/Devonshire+House+Fancy+Dress+Ball+Album (accessed 3 April 2021).
33 museumsandgalleries.leeds.gov.uk/leeds-museums/abbey-house-museum/the-childrens-fancy-dress-ball/ (accessed 3 April 2021).
34 London 1999, pp. 112–8; Riding 2006, pp. 46–9.
35 In her journal, Queen Victoria wrote, 'I feel a sort of reverence in going over these scenes in this most beautiful country, which I am proud to call my own, where there was such devoted loyalty to the family of my ancestors – for Stuart blood is in my veins, and I am now their representative, and the people are as devoted and loyal to me as they were to that unhappy race.' Worthington 1884, vol. 2, p. 197.
36 See Ross Finocchio, 'The One that Got Away: Holbein's *Christina of Denmark* and British Portraits in The Frick Collection', in Reist 2014, pp. 181–94.
37 Subtitle of article in *The Times*, 24 January 1922; see National Gallery Archive (hereafter NGA), NG24/1922/1: Press cuttings, January–March 1922: 7. Loans In: Duveen, Gainsborough 'The Blue Boy'.
38 *Daily Mail*, 3 January 1922, press cutting preserved in NGA, NG24/1922/1.
39 *Daily Graphic*, 4 January 1922, press cutting preserved in NGA, NG24/1922/1.

Testament of Youth

1 Cited in S. Bennett, 'The Formation of Henry Huntington's Collection of British Paintings' in Asleson and Bennett 2001, p. 5.
2 Henry Huntington to Duveen Brothers, Paris, 7 October 1921. Duveen Scrapbook, 23 B, Huntington Library.
3 Sloman 2013. See also Sloman 2004. Evidence, however, remains inconclusive. See London 2018a, p. 33.
4 Reproduced in Belsey and Wright 2002, p. 23.
5 For a description of the pantomime, see Hedquist 2020, pp. 91–2. For more on *The Blue Boy* in nineteenth-century British popular culture, see ibid., pp. 82–97.
6 'A Farewell,' *The Times*, London, 27 January 1922, p. 13, clipping enclosed with letter from Andrew Mellon to Henry Huntington, 1924. Henry Edwards Huntington papers, Huntington Library, mssHEH 8903.
7 For more on *The Blue Boy* as a symbol of loss, see K. Salatino, 'Foreword', in Hess and M. McCurdy 2015, p. 11.
8 See Hedquist 2020, p. 24. For more on the reception of Van Dyck after his death, see London 2009.
9 The painting actually left the Royal Collection twice. After having been sold in 1650, it was reacquired by Charles II, only to leave the collection again under James II.
10 'Mr Gainsborough, the Painter,' *British Mercury*, vol. 6, no. 35 (1788), p. 273.
11 Boyle 1885, no. 8.
12 Hedquist 2020, p. 112.
13 *The Blue Boy Blues*, words and music by Cole Porter, 1922.
14 'A Farewell', *The Times*, London, 27 January 1922, p. 13.
15 See Bennett in Asleson and Bennett 2001, p. 5.
16 Bennett 2013, fig. 2.31, p. 91.
17 For more on Henry and Arabella Huntington's relationship, see ibid., pp. 131–256.
18 See Bennett in Asleson and Bennett 2001, pp. 7–8.
19 Ibid., p. 222.
20 Bennett in Asleson and Bennett 2001, pp. 2–3.
21 Quoted in Kopper et al. 2016, p. 19.
22 For more on Paul Mellon's collection, see New Haven and London 2007.
23 Quoted in Hedquist 2020, p. 121.
24 Ibid., p. 122.
25 For a detailed list of productions featuring *The Blue Boy*, see ibid., pp. 128–37.
26 These include posters, postcards, figurines, paint-by-numbers kits, pillowcases, ashtrays and other home decor. The Huntington Art Museum houses a collection of these items, some of which are illustrated in McCurdy 2021, fig. 4, p. 18.
27 Tomkins 1980, p. 19.
28 Quoted in Hobbs 2011, p. 23.

Cat. 1: *The Blue Boy*, about 1770

1 See Belsey 2019 vol. 1, nos 288, 290, 382 and 436.
2 Asleson and Bennett 2001, pp. 104–8. For a suggested identity for the figure, see Sloman 2013, pp. 231–7.
3 Malone 1797, vol. 1, p. xvi.
4 Kidson 2015, vol. II, no. 1164.
5 London 2018a, cat. 23.
6 Asleson and Bennett 2001, p. 107.
7 For more on how artists employed such strategies to stand out in the environment of the Royal Academy exhibition, see Hallett et al. 2018.
8 Reynolds 1992, p. 198.
9 Brenneman 2003, pp. 80–95.
10 Ibid., pp. 84–5 and Belsey 2019, vol. 1, pp. 278–80.

Cat. 2: *Mr and Mrs William Hallett ('The Morning Walk')*, 1785

1 Egerton 1998, p. 122.
2 Ibid.
3 Hayes 2001, p. 174.
4 London 2002, p. 270.
5 Belsey 2019, vol. 2, p. 752.
6 Brenneman 2003, p. 82.
7 Ibid.

Cat. 3: *Elizabeth and Mary Linley*, about 1772

1 *London Chronicle*, 5–7 May 1772.
2 For example, Antoine Watteau, *The Scale of Love*, probably 1717–18. National Gallery, London (NG2897). For the Stuart court masque tradition, see Orgel and Strong 1973.
3 A 'Spanish guitar, curiously inlaid' was listed among the artist's possessions at Christie's, 10 May 1799, lot 114. London 1988, p. 63. For Gainsborough's musical life, see Asfour and Williamson 1999b pp. 146–94 and Sloman 2002, pp. 100–6.
4 A recent restoration treatment removed the additions of clothing but kept the alterations to the women's hair. Belsey 2019, vol. 2, p. 555, no. 590.
5 Reynolds 1992, p. 307.
6 Belsey 2019, vol. 1, pp. 346–7, no. 360.
7 Letter from Gainsborough to William Jackson, dated Bath, 4 June, year unknown, Hayes 2001, p. 68. Belsey 2019, pp. 347–8, no. 360. London 2018a, p. 55, p. 140, no. 30.
8 Sloman 2002, p. 191; London 2018a, pp. 23, p. 43.
9 Tristram also appears in the drawing *Tristram and Fox* (about 1770, private collection), London 2018a, p. 125, no. 23. See Sloman 2013, p. 236; Asleson and Bennett 2001, p. 110, note 22.

Cat. 4: *Lord John Stuart and his Brother, Lord Bernard Stuart*, about 1638

1 John died of wounds received at the Battle of Cheriton, 29 March 1644, and Bernard died in battle during the siege of Chester in September 1645. *DNB* 1908–9, vol. 19, pp. 73 and 108.
2 Egerton in London and Antwerp 1999, p. 320, no. 97.
3 This copy, measuring 235 x 146.1 cm, is today in the Saint Louis Art Museum, Missouri. See Belsey 2019 vol. 2, pp. 1005–6, no. 1090. It is generally thought that this copy was painted in the 1760s, although it has also been suggested that Gainsborough may have studied the painting when he made a portrait of the 4th Earl of Darnley in 1785. See Wark 1974, p. 45.
4 Belsey 2019 vol. 1, pp. 184–5, no. 182.
5 *Discourse XIV*, a lecture delivered to students of the Royal Academy, 10 December 1788. Reynolds 1992, p. 308.
6 Richardson 1715, p. 24. Sloman notes that Gainsborough echoes Richardson's views on Van Dyck in his correspondence. Sloman 2002, p. 160.
7 London 2018a, p. 114, no. 18, fig. 34.

Cat. 5: *George Villiers, 2nd Duke of Buckingham (1628–1687) and Lord Francis Villiers (1629–1648)*, 1635

1 Larsen 1988, vol. 1, p. 325.
2 Ibid., vol. 2, p. 309, no. 779.
3 Ibid., vol. 2, p. 400, no. 1023.
4 Oliver Millar was the first to suggest this. Millar 1963, no. 153.
5 Belsey 2019, vol. 1, pp. 340–1, no. 356; London 2018a, pp. 46–7, 95, no. 9.
6 Johan Joseph Zoffany, *George, Prince of Wales, and Frederick, later Duke of York, at Buckingham House*, 1765 (Royal Collection).
7 Numerous copies of this mezzotint survive, for example at the British Museum (1838,0420.184). James McArdell was an Irish mezzotint engraver, who worked closely with Sir Joshua Reynolds from 1754. See Goodwin 1903.
8 London 2018a, pp. 45–7. See also Pointon 1998.

Cat. 6: *Mrs Siddons*, 1785

1 *ODNB*, vol. 50, pp. 515–22.
2 Mannings 2000, vol. 1, pp. 414–5, no. 1619. See also Los Angeles 1999.
3 Belsey 2019, vol. 2, p. 762–4, no. 817.
4 Records of her performances indicate she was in London from 5 October 1784 until 18 May 1785. The drawing is at the Cleveland Museum of Art. Hayes 1970, vol. 1, pp. 128–9, no. 64.
5 Belsey 2019, vol. 2, p. 762–4, no. 817.
6 See Egerton 1998, p. 118.
7 *Morning Herald*, 30 March 1785.
8 Wind 1986, p. 46; Rosenthal 1999, p. 151; Simon 1987, pp. 65–6; Asfour and Williamson 1999a, p. 38.
9 Simon 1987, p. 66. For Reynolds's picture see Mannings 2000, vol. 1, pp. 146–7, no. 420.

Cat. 7: *Portrait of Charles William Lambton ('The Red Boy')*, 1825

1 Lawrence's poem read 'Proceed, dear boy, and climb the hill/Enjoy the morning of thy time/And all the rocks of future life/ As cheerful and as active climb.' See Levey 2005, p. 258.
2 For Lawrence's drawings collection, see Joannides 2007, pp. 1–45.
3 London 2010, pp. 94–7, no. 2; Levey 2005, pp. 84–90.
4 London 2010, pp. 105–7.
5 Asleson and Bennett 2001, p. 242, no. 50. The Barrett family was one of the wealthiest families in Jamaica, owning over 84,000 acres and 2,000 enslaved Africans by the mid-eighteenth century. See Barrett 2000.
6 The sitter's identity was uncovered in 1927, and the painting had been known as *'Pinkie'* from at least 1907. Asleson and Bennett 2001, p. 247, note 39.
7 *Illustrated London News*, 27 May 1922, p. 20.
8 Secrest 2005, p. 200.
9 'The story of how Master Lambton was first painted as a "Yellow Boy" may be supplemented by quoting the popular ditty about the "yellow dandy" – the young sitter's father, John George Lambton, afterwards 1st Earl of Durham: "Mr. Lambton leads the van/Pleasant fellow, pleasant fellow/Looking quite the gentleman/Rather yellow, rather yellow"'. *Yorkshire Post and Leeds Intelligencer*, 8 April 1932, p. 6.
10 For example, *The Children of John Angerstein* (1807), Garlick 1989, p. 138, no. 32, and *Frances Hawkins and her Son, John James Hamilton* (1805–6), Garlick 1989, p. 234, no. 536. See Pointon in London 2010, pp. 63–4, 72–3.
11 London 2010, pp. 72–3.

Bibliography

ASFOUR AND WILLIAMSON 1999a
A. Asfour and P. Williamson, 'Gainsborough's Mrs Siddons: The woman as artist', *British Art Journal*, vol. 1, no. 1, Autumn 1999, pp. 38–44

ASFOUR AND WILLIAMSON 1999b
A. Asfour and P. Williamson, *Gainsborough's Vision*, Liverpool 1999

ASLESON AND BENNETT 2001
R. Asleson and S. Bennett, *British Paintings at The Huntington*, New Haven and London 2001

BARRETT 2000
R.A. Barrett, *The Barretts of Jamaica: The Family of Elizabeth Barrett Browning*, Athlone 2000

BELLHOUSE 1857
E.T. Bellhouse, *What to See, and Where to See it! Or, The Operative's Guide to the Art Treasures Exhibition*, Manchester 1857

BELSEY 2019
H. Belsey, *Thomas Gainsborough: The Portraits, Fancy Pictures and Copies after Old Masters*, 2 vols, New Haven and London 2019

BELSEY AND WRIGHT 2002
H. Belsey and C. Wright, *Gainsborough Pop*, London and Sudbury 2002

BENNETT 2013
S. Bennett, *The Art of Wealth: The Huntingtons in the Gilded Age*, San Marino 2013

BOLD 1998
J. Bold, *Wilton House and English Palladianism*, London 1998

BOYLE 1885
M.L. Boyle, *Biographical Catalogue of the Portraits at Panshanger, the Seat of Earl Cowper, K.G.*, 1885, no. 8

BRENNEMAN 2003
D.A. Brenneman, 'Thomas Gainsborough and the "thin brilliant Style of Pencilling of Vandyke"', *Huntington Library Quarterly*, vol. 66, nos 1–2, 2003, pp. 81–95

BURKE 1955
J. Burke (ed.), W. Hogarth, *The Analysis of Beauty with Rejected Passage and Autobiographical Notes*, Oxford 1955

CUNNINGHAM 1830
A. Cunningham, *The Lives of the Most Eminent British Painters, Sculptors and Architects*, 2nd edn, London 1830, vol. 1

DNB 1908–9
Dictionary of National Biography, 2nd edn, 22 vols, London 1908–9

EGERTON 1998
J. Egerton, *National Gallery Catalogues: The British School*, London 1998

EINBERG 2016
E. Einberg, *William Hogarth: A Complete Catalogue of Paintings*, New Haven and London 2016

GARLICK 1989
K. Garlick, *Sir Thomas Lawrence: A Complete Catalogue of the Oil Paintings*, London 1989

GOODWIN 1903
G. Goodwin, *British Mezzotinters: James McArdell*, London 1903

HALLET AND RIDING 2006
M. Hallet and C. Riding, *Hogarth*, London 2006

HALLET ET AL. 2018
M. Hallett et al. (eds), *The Royal Academy of Arts Summer Exhibition: A Chronicle, 1769–2018*, at https://chronicle250.com/1769

HART 2011
V. Hart, *Inigo Jones: The Architect of Kings*, New Haven and London 2011

HAYES 1963
J. Hayes, 'Gainsborough and Rubens', *Apollo*, August 1963, pp. 89–97

HAYES 1970
J. Hayes, *The Drawings of Thomas Gainsborough*, 2 vols, London 1970

HAYES 2001
J. Hayes (ed.), *The Letters of Thomas Gainsborough*, New Haven and London 2001

HEDQUIST 2020
V. Hedquist, *Class, Gender, and Sexuality in Thomas Gainsborough's* Blue Boy, London and New York 2020

HESS AND MCCURDY 2015
C. Hess and M. McCurdy, *Blue Boy & Co.: European Art at The Huntington*, Munich, London and New York 2015

HOBBS 2011
R. Hobbs, 'Kehinde Wiley's Conceptual Realism' in *Kehinde Wiley*, New York 2011

HOPKINS 1991
J. Hopkins, '"Such a Twin Likeness there was in the Pair": An Investigation into the Painting of the Cholmondeley Sisters', *Transactions of the Historic Society of Lancashire and Cheshire*, vol. 141, 1991, pp. 1–37

IRELAND 1857
A. Ireland, *The Art-Treasures Examiner: A Pictorial, Critical, and Historical Record of the Art Treasures Exhibition at Manchester in 1857*, Manchester 1857

JAMESON 1844
A. Jameson, *Companion to the Most Celebrated Private Galleries of Art in London*, London 1844

JOANNIDES 2007
P. Joannides, *The Drawings of Michelangelo and his Followers in the Ashmolean Museum*, Cambridge 2007

KIDSON 2015
A. Kidson, *George Romney: A Complete Catalogue of his Paintings*, New Haven and London 2015

KOPPER ET AL. 2016
P. Kopper, et al., *America's National Gallery of Art*, Princeton and Oxford 2016

LARSEN 1988
E. Larsen, *The Paintings of Anthony Van Dyck*, 2 vols, Freren 1988

LEVEY 2005
M. Levey, *Sir Thomas Lawrence*, New Haven and London 2005

LIVERPOOL, LONDON AND SAN MARINO 2002
A. Kidson, *George Romney, 1734–1802*, exh. cat., Walker Art Gallery, Liverpool; National Portrait Gallery, London; The Huntington Library, Art Collections, and Botanical Gardens, San Marino 2002

LONDON 1981
D. Gordon, *Second Sight: Rubens, The Watering Place, Gainsborough, The Watering Place*, exh. cat., The National Gallery, London 1981

LONDON 1988
A Nest of Nightingales: Thomas Gainsborough, the Linley Sisters, exh. cat., Dulwich Picture Gallery, London 1988

LONDON 1999
P. Funnell and M. Warner (eds), *Millais: Portraits*, exh. cat., National Portrait Gallery, London 1999

LONDON 2002
M. Rosenthal and M. Myrone (eds), *Gainsborough*, exh. cat., Tate, London 2002

LONDON 2003
P. Noon and S. Bann, *Constable to Delacroix: British Art and the French Romantics*, exh. cat., Tate, London 2003

LONDON 2005
M. Postle (ed.), *Joshua Reynolds: The Creation of Celebrity*, exh. cat., Tate, London 2005

LONDON 2009
K. Hearn, *Van Dyck and Britain*, exh. cat., Tate, London 2009

LONDON 2010
C. Albinson and P. Funnell (eds), *Thomas Lawrence: Regency Power and Brilliance*, exh. cat., National Portrait Gallery, London 2010

LONDON 2018a
D.H. Solkin, A. Bermingham and S. Sloman, *Gainsborough's Family Album*, exh. cat., National Portrait Gallery, London 2018

LONDON 2018b
Charles I: King and Collector, exh. cat., Royal Academy of Arts, London 2018

LONDON AND ANTWERP 1999
C. Brown and H. Vlieghe, *Van Dyck, 1599–1641*, exh. cat., Royal Academy, London; Koninklijk Museum voor Schone Kunsten, Antwerp 1999

LONDON AND DÜSSELDORF 2020
B. Baumgärtel (ed.), *Angelica Kauffman*, exh. cat., Royal Academy of Arts, London; Kunstpalast Düsseldorf 2020

LONDON AND ROME 1996
A. Wilton and I. Bignamini, *Grand Tour: Lure of Italy in the Eighteenth Century*, exh. cat., Tate, London; Palazzo delle Esposizioni, Rome 1996

LOS ANGELES 1999
R. Asleson (ed.), *A Passion for Performance: Sarah Siddons and her Portraitists*, exh. cat., J. Paul Getty Museum, Los Angeles 1999

MACDONALD 1995
M.F. MacDonald, *James McNeill Whistler: Drawings, Pastels and Watercolours. A Catalogue Raisonné*, New Haven and London 1995

MACLAREN YOUNG ET AL. 1980
A. Maclaren Young et al., *The Paintings of James McNeill Whistler*, New Haven and London 1980

MALONE 1797
E. Malone, 'Some Account of the Life and Writings of Sir Joshua Reynolds', in *The Works of Sir Joshua Reynolds, Knt., Late President of the Royal Academy*, London 1797, vol. 1, p. xvi

MANNINGS 2000
D. Mannings, *Sir Joshua Reynolds: A Complete Catalogue of his Paintings*, 2 vols, New Haven and London 2000

MCCURDY 2021
M. McCurdy (ed.), *Kehinde Wiley: Portrait of a Young Gentleman*, San Marino 2021

MILLAR 1963
O. Millar, *The Tudor, Stuart and Early Georgian Pictures in the Royal Collection*, 2 vols, London 1963

MOWL AND EARNSHAW 1988
T. Mowl and B. Earnshaw, *John Wood: Architect of Obsession*, Bath 1988

NEW HAVEN AND LONDON 2007
J. Baskett et al., *Paul Mellon's Legacy: A Passion for British Art*, exh. cat., Royal Academy of Arts, London; Yale Center for British Art, New Haven 2007

ODNB
Oxford Dictionary of National Biography, 60 vols, London 2004

ORGEL AND STRONG 1973
S. Orgel and R. Strong, *Inigo Jones: The Theatre of the Stuart Court*, 2 vols, Berkeley 1973

ORMOND AND KILMURRAY 2002
R. Ormond and E. Kilmurray, *John Singer Sargent*, New Haven and London 2002, vol. 2

PASSAVANT 1836
J.D. Passavant, *Tour of a German Artist in England: With Notices of Private Galleries, and Remarks on the State of Art*, 2 vols, London 1836

Pointon 1998
M. Pointon, *Hanging the Head: Portraiture and Social Formation in Eighteenth-Century England*, New Haven and London 1998

Postle 1995
M. Postle, *Sir Joshua Reynolds: The Subject Paintings*, Cambridge 1995

Postle 2011
M. Postle, *Johann Zoffany RA: Society Observed*, exh. cat., Royal Academy of Arts, London; Yale Center for British Art, New Haven 2011

Reist 2014
I. Reist (ed.), *British Models of Art Collecting and the American Response: Reflections across the Pond*, Burlington, VT and Farnham 2014

Retford 2017
K. Retford, *The Conversation Piece: Making Modern Art in Eighteenth-Century Britain*, New Haven and London 2017

Reynolds 1891
J. Reynolds, *Discourses*, ed. E. Gilpin Johnson, Chicago 1891

Reynolds 1992
J. Reynolds, *Discourses*, ed. P. Rogers, London 1992

Ribeiro 1995
A. Ribeiro, *The Art of Dress: Fashion in England and France, 1750–1820*, New Haven and London 1995

Richardson 1715
J. Richardson, *An Essay on the Theory of Painting*, London 1715

Riding 2004
C. Riding, 'Old Masters and Edwardian Society' in *The Edwardian: Secrets and Desires*, exh. cat., National Gallery of Australia, Canberra; Art Gallery of South Australia, Adelaide, Canberra 2004

Riding 2006
C. Riding, *John Everett Millais*, London 2006

Riding 2012
J. Riding, *Joseph Highmore, 1692–1780*, doctoral thesis, University of York, 2012, vol. 1

Riding 2016
J. Riding, *Jacobites: A New History of the '45 Rebellion*, London 2016

Riding 2017
J. Riding, *Basic Instincts: Love, Passion and Violence in the Art of Joseph Highmore*, London 2017

Riding 2021
J. Riding, *Hogarth: A Life in Progress*, London 2021

Rosenthal 1999
M. Rosenthal, *The Art of Thomas Gainsborough*, New Haven and London 1999

Secrest 2005
M. Secrest, *Duveen: A Life in Art*, New York 2005

Simon 1987
R. Simon, *The Portrait in Britain and America*, Oxford 1987

Sloman 2002
S. Sloman, *Gainsborough in Bath*, New Haven and London 2002

Sloman 2004
S. Sloman, '"A Divine Countenance": Gainsborough's Portrait of his Nephew Rediscovered', *Burlington Magazine*, vol. 146, no. 1214 (2004), pp. 319–22

Sloman 2013
S. Sloman, 'Gainsborough's "Blue Boy"', *Burlington Magazine*, vol. 155, no. 1321 (April 2013), pp. 231–7

Smart 1992
A. Smart, *Allan Ramsay: Painter, Essayist and Man of the Enlightenment*, New Haven and London 1992

Sudbury 2006
D. Perkins, *Gainsborough's Dogs*, exh. cat., Gainsborough's House, Sudbury 2006

Sudbury 2018
M. Bills and R. Jones, *Early Gainsborough: 'From the Obscurity of a Country Town'*, exh. cat., Gainsborough's House, Sudbury 2018

Tomkins 1980
C. Tomkins, *Off the Wall: Robert Rauschenberg and the Art World of Our Time*, New York 1980

Vaughan 2002
W. Vaughan, *Gainsborough*, London 2002

Waagen 1854
G.F. Waagen, trans. Lady Elizabeth Rigby Eastlake, *Treasures of Art in Great Britain: Being an Account of the Chief Collections of Paintings, Drawings, Sculptures, Illuminated Mss., &c.*, 3 vols, London 1854

Wark 1974
R.R. Wark, 'A Note on Gainsborough and Van Dyck', *Museum Monographs III, Papers on Objects in the Collections of City Art Museum of Saint Louis,* St Louis 1974, pp. 45–53

Way 1912
T.R. Way, *Memories of James McNeill Whistler, the Artist*, London 1912

Whitley 1930
W.T. Whitley, *Art in England, 1821–1837*, Cambridge 1930

Wind 1986
E. Wind, *Hume and the Heroic Portrait: Studies in Eighteenth-Century Imagery*, ed. J. Anderson, Oxford 1986

Woodall 1963
M. Woodall (ed.), *The Letters of Thomas Gainsborough*, London 1963

Worthington 1884
R. Worthington, *More Leaves from the Journal of a Life in the Highlands: From 1862 to 1882*, 2 vols, New York 1884

Acknowledgements

In addition to the comments made in Gabriele Finaldi's foreword, I would like to add my own heartfelt thanks to Christina Nielsen, Melinda McCurdy and Janet Alberti at the Huntington and to colleagues who supported us in securing loans to the exhibition: Tim Knox, Desmond Shawe-Taylor at the Royal Collection Trust, and Jennifer Scott at Dulwich Picture Gallery.

At the National Gallery, I am especially grateful to Jane Knowles and Katherine Miller for their support and management of the exhibition, and to Olivia Threlkeld and Rebekah Barlow, as well as Nicola Smith and Louise Nyborg for their sensitive exhibition design. The accompanying catalogue has been a truly collaborative effort, designed by Joe Ewart and edited by Rachel Giles, and overseen with care and attention by Laura Lappin, Diana Adell, Jane Hyne, Suzanne Bosman, Rebecca Thornton and other colleagues at the National Gallery Company. I am also grateful to Susanna Avery-Quash, Melinda McCurdy, Jacqueline Riding and Imogen Tedbury for their insightful contributions to the catalogue, and for their advice and support throughout. Finally, I would like to acknowledge the following individuals for their assistance in matters relating to the exhibition and catalogue: Tabitha Barber, Caroline Campbell, Juliet Carey, Neil Evans, Tracy Jones, Joseph Kendra, Alexandra Moskalenko, Patrick O'Sullivan and Belinda Phillpot.

Christine Riding
The National Gallery, London

List of Lenders

London
Dulwich Picture Gallery

London
The National Gallery

London
Royal Collection Trust

San Marino, CA
The Huntington Library, Art Museum, and Botanical Gardens

Photographic Credits

Blenheim Palace, Oxfordshire
© Blenheim Palace, Oxfordshire / Bridgeman Images: fig. 17.

Edinburgh
© National Galleries of Scotland: fig. 11.

Fort Worth, Texas
© Kimbell Art Museum, Fort Worth, Texas: fig. 16.

Holkham, Norfolk
© By kind permission of the Earl of Leicester and the Trustees of the Holkham Estate / Bridgeman Images: fig. 8.

Leeds
© Leeds Museums and Galleries / Leeds Museums and Galleries, UK / Bridgeman Images: fig. 20.

Liverpool
© National Museums Liverpool / Bridgeman Images: figs 6, 21.

London
© By Permission of the Trustees of the Dulwich Picture Gallery, London: cat. 3.
© IWM Q 45825: fig. 25.
© The National Gallery, London: cats 2, 4, 6, 7; figs 1, 34, 37.
© Peter Blake / photo Tate: fig. 30.
Royal Collection Trust / © Her Majesty Queen Elizabeth II 2022: cat. 5; figs 2, 9, 19, 23. © Tate: fig. 33.
© By kind permission of the Trustees of the Wallace Collection, London / Bridgeman Images: fig. 15.

Los Angeles, California
© Los Angeles County Museum of Art, California: fig. 10.

New York
© Copyright The Frick Collection, New York: figs 26, 28.

Private collections
© Painters / Alamy Stock Photo: fig. 14.
© Bridgeman Images: fig. 35.
© Christie's Images / Bridgeman Images: fig. 22.
© Alex Israel / photo Joshua White: fig. 31
© Mary Evans Picture Library: fig. 13.

Saint Louis, Missouri
© The Saint Louis Art Museum, Missouri: fig. 5.

San Marino, California
© courtesy of the Huntington Library, Art Museum, and Botanical Gardens, San Marino, California: cat. 1; figs 24, 27, 38, 39.
© Kehinde Wiley / photo courtesy of the Huntington Library, Art Museum, and Botanical Gardens, San Marino, California: fig. 32.

Waddesdon
© Waddesdon Image Library: figs 7, 18.

Washington, DC
© Freer Gallery of Art: fig. 12.
Courtesy National Gallery of Art, Washington: fig. 29.

Wilton House
© Collection of the Earl of Pembroke, Wilton House, Wilts / Bridgeman Images: fig. 3.

Wolverhampton
© Wolverhampton Art Gallery / Bridgeman Images: fig. 4.

Worcester, Massachusetts
© Worcester Art Museum / Bridgeman Images: fig. 36.